NURSERY DECOR *for beginners*

CREATIVE
PUBLISHING
international

MINNETONKA, MINNESOTA

Copyright © 2000
Creative Publishing international, Inc.
5900 Green Oak Drive
Minnetonka, Minnesota 55343
1-800-328-3895
All rights reserved
Printed in U.S.A.

President/CEO: David D. Murphy
Vice President/Editorial: Patricia K. Jacobsen
Vice President/Retail Sales & Marketing: Richard M. Miller

Executive Editor: Elaine Perry
Project Manager: Linnéa Christensen
Senior Editor: Linda Neubauer
Senior Art Director: Stephanie Michaud
Desktop Publishing Specialist: Laurie Kristensen
Researcher: Carol Olson
Project & Prop Stylist: Joanne Wawra
Sewing Staff: Arlene Dohrman, Sheila Duffy, Joanne Wawra
Technical Photo Stylists: Arlene Dohrman, Kathleen Smith, Joanne Wawra
Studio Services Manager: Marcia Chambers
Photo Services Coordinator: Carol Osterhus
Director of Photography: Chuck Nields
Photographers: Tate Carlson, Andrea Rugg
Photography Assistant: Kevin Heddin
Director of Production Services: Kim Gerber
Production Manager: Stasia Dorn
Contributors: Coats & Clark Inc., Olfa® Products International

NURSERY DECOR FOR BEGINNERS created by:
The Editors of Creative Publishing international, Inc.

Printed on American paper by:
  R. R. Donnelley & Sons Co.
10 9 8 7 6 5 4 3 2 1

Creative Publishing international, Inc. offers a variety of how-to books.
For information write:
    Creative Publishing international, Inc.
      Subscriber Books
    5900 Green Oak Drive
    Minnetonka, MN 55343

Library of Congress Cataloging-in-Publication Data

Nursery decor for beginners.
        p. cm. -- (Seams sew easy)
      At head of title: Coats & Clark.
      Includes index.
      ISBN 0-86573-866-1
      1. Household linens. 2. Nurseries--Equipment and supplies. 3. Infants' supplies. I.
    Title: Coats & Clark nursery decor for beginners. II. Coats & Clark. III. Series.

TT387 .N87 2000
646.2'1--dc21   99-088292

Coats & Clark

NURSERY DECOR *for beginners*

Contents

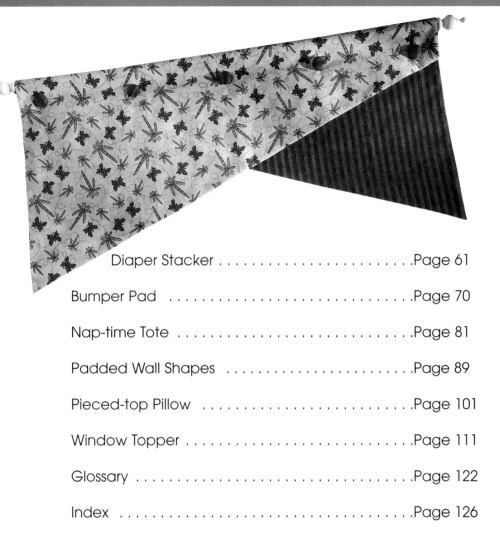

How to *Use This Book*

Welcome to the rewarding world of sewing. The *Seams Sew Easy™* series of books is designed to encourage creativity and instill confidence as you learn to sew. Easy-to-follow instructions with colorful photographs and illustrations help you build your sewing skills while making home decorating and apparel items that are as useful as they are appealing.

Planning and decorating your baby's nursery can be exciting and fun. However, the expense can really skyrocket, especially if you want a custom decorator look. By sewing the nursery decor items yourself, you are able to get exactly what you want at a fraction of the cost. Many items are amazingly easy to create! This book will teach you how to sew them and, in the process, you'll develop sewing skills that will help you tackle many other sewing projects with confidence.

The projects in this book have been designed to guide you from your first nervous stitch at your sewing machine to comfortable familiarity. Each project will teach you new skills, listed under WHAT YOU'LL LEARN. Throughout the book you will find tips and explanations to help you understand the "why" behind what you are doing. We have also shown variations for many of the projects, encouraging you to explore the unlimited possibilities for design and fabric choices.

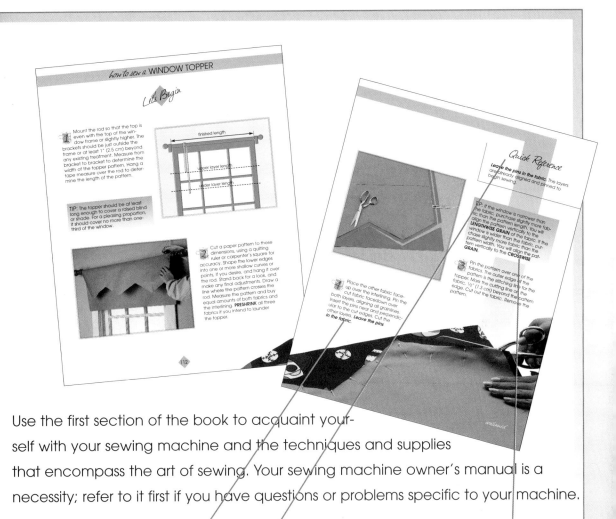

Use the first section of the book to acquaint yourself with your sewing machine and the techniques and supplies
that encompass the art of sewing. Your sewing machine owner's manual is a
necessity; refer to it first if you have questions or problems specific to your machine.

The first step in any sewing project is to read through the directions from beginning
to end. Refer to the **Quick Reference** for definitions or elaborations on any word or
phrases printed **like this** on the page. If the word or phrase is followed by a page
number, its reference can be found on that page. Words printed **LIKE THIS** can be
found in the **GLOSSARY** on page 122. At the beginning of every project you will
find a list telling you WHAT YOU'LL NEED. Read through the information on fabrics
before you go shopping, so the fabric store will seem a little more user-friendly
when you get there.

Above all, enjoy the process. Give yourself the opportunity to be creative, and sew
up the nursery of your dreams!

The Sewing Machine

The principle parts common to all modern sewing machines are shown in the diagrams at right. The parts may look different on your model, and they may have slightly different locations, so open your owner's manual, also. If you do not have an owner's manual for your machine, you should be able to get one from a sewing machine dealer who sells your brand. Become familiar with the names of the parts and their functions. As you spend more time sewing, these items will become second nature to you.

If you are buying a new machine, consider how much and what kind of sewing you expect to do. Talk to friends who sew and to sales personnel. Ask for demonstrations, and sew on the machine yourself. Experiment with the various features while sewing on a variety of fabrics, including knits, wovens, lightweights, and denim. Think about the optional features of the machine and which ones you want on yours. Many dealers offer free sewing lessons with the purchase of a machine. Take advantage! These lessons will be geared to your particular brand and model of sewing machine.

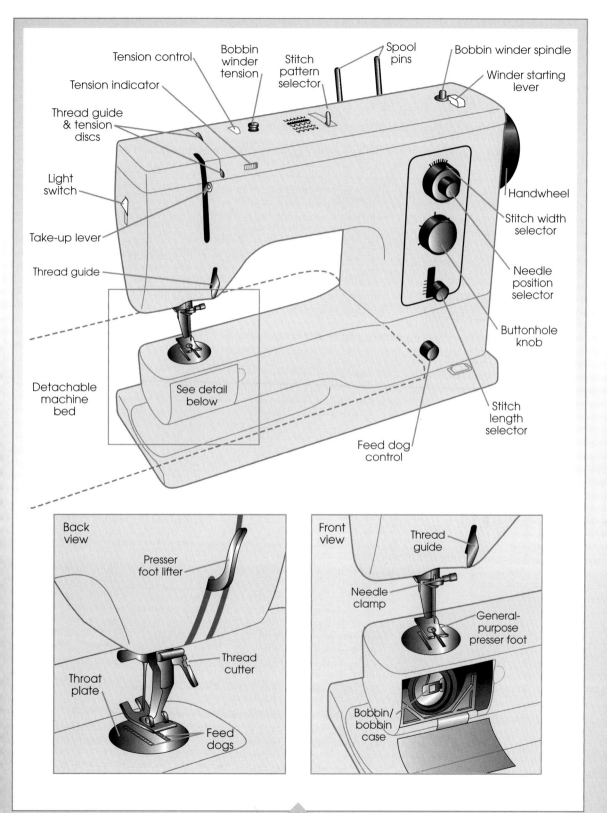

Tension control

Bobbin winder tension

Stitch pattern selector

Spool pins

Bobbin winder spindle

Winder starting lever

Tension indicator

Thread guide & tension discs

Light switch

Take-up lever

Thread guide

Detachable machine bed

See detail below

Handwheel

Stitch width selector

Needle position selector

Buttonhole knob

Stitch length selector

Feed dog control

Back view

Presser foot lifter

Throat plate

Thread cutter

Feed dogs

Front view

Thread guide

Needle clamp

General-purpose presser foot

Bobbin/ bobbin case

Machine *Accessories*

Sewing Machine Needles

Sewing machine needles come in a variety of styles and sizes. The correct needle choice depends mostly on the fabric you have selected. Sharp points **(A)**, used for woven fabrics, are designed to pierce the fabric. Ballpoints **(B)** are designed to slip between the loops of knit fabric rather than pierce and possibly damage the fabric. Universal points **(C)** are designed to work on both woven and knitted fabrics. The size of the needle is designated by a number, generally given in both European (60, 70, 80, 90, 100, 110) and American (9, 11, 12, 14, 16, 18) numbering systems. Use size 11/70 or 12/80 needles for any of the mediumweight fabrics you would find suitable for the projects in this book. A larger number means the needle is thicker and that it is appropriate for use with heavier fabrics and heavier threads.

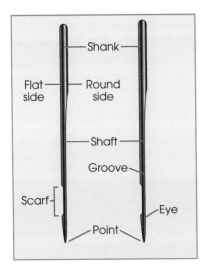

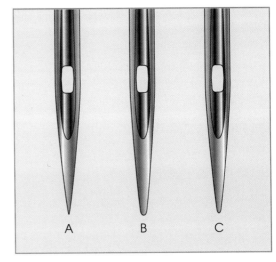

TIP: Though needle style and size are usually indicated in some way on the needle, it is often difficult to see without a magnifying glass, and you most likely will not remember what needle is in the machine. As an easy reminder, when you finish a sewing session, leave a fabric swatch from your current project under the presser foot.

Bobbins

Stitches are made by locking the upper thread with a lower thread, carried on a bobbin. Always use bobbins in the correct style and size for your machine. Bobbin thread tension is controlled by a spring on the bobbin case, which may be built in **(A)** or removable **(B).**

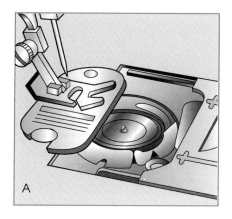

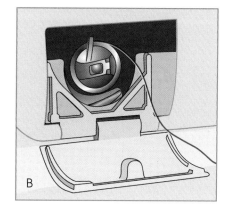

Presser Feet

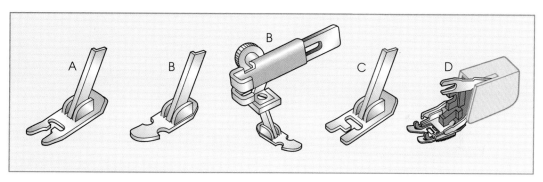

Every sewing machine comes with accessories for specialized tasks. More can be purchased as you develop your interest and skills. Your machine manual or dealer can show you what accessories are available and will explain how to use them to get the best results.

A general-purpose foot **(A),** probably the one you will use most often, has a wide opening to accommodate the side-to-side movement of the needle in all types of utility (nondecorative) stitches. It is also suitable for most straight stitching. A zipper foot **(B)** is used to insert zippers or to stitch

any seam that has more bulk on one side than the other. For some sewing machines, the zipper foot is stationary, requiring you to move the needle position to the right or left. For other styles, the position of the zipper foot itself is adjustable. A special-purpose or embroidery foot **(C)** has a grooved bottom that allows the foot to ride smoothly over decorative stitches or raised cords. Some styles are clear plastic, allowing you to see your work more clearly. An Even Feed® foot **(D)** feeds top and bottom layers at equal rates, allowing you to more easily match patterns or stitch bulky layers, as in quilted projects.

Getting *Ready to Sew*

Simple tasks of inserting the needle, winding the bobbin, and threading the machine have tremendous influence on the stitch quality and performance of your machine. Use this guide as a general reference, but refer to your owner's manual for instructions specific to your machine.

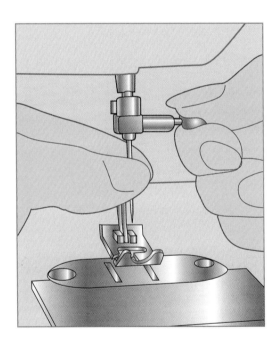 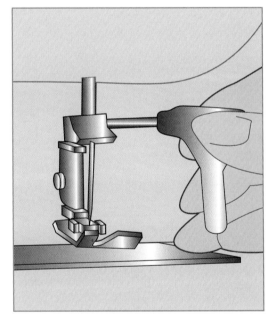

Inserting the Needle

Loosen the needle clamp. After selecting the appropriate needle for your project (page 10), insert it into the machine as high as it will go. The grooved side of the needle faces forward, if your bobbin gets inserted from the front or top; it faces to the left, if your bobbin gets inserted on the left. Tighten the clamp securely.

Winding the Bobbin

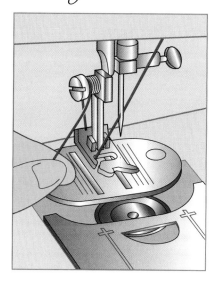

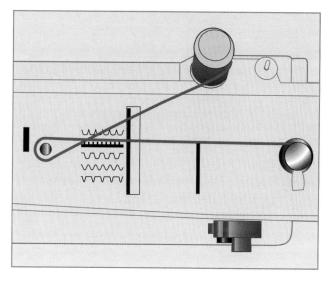

If the bobbin case is built in, the bobbin is wound in place with the machine fully threaded as if to sew (page 14).

Removable bobbins are wound on the top or side of the machine, with the machine threaded for bobbin winding, as described in your owner's manual.

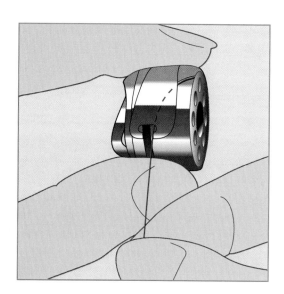

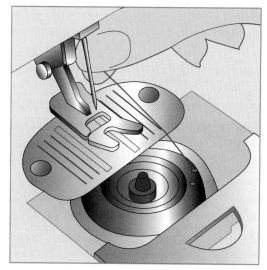

Bobbin thread must be drawn through the bobbin case tension spring. For wind-in-place bobbins, this happens automatically when you wind the bobbin, but you must do it manually when you insert a bobbin that already has thread on it.

continued

Threading the Machine

Because every sewing machine is different, the threading procedure for your machine may differ slightly from the one shown here. Once again, it is important to refer to your owner's manual. Every upper thread guide adds a little tension to the thread as it winds its way to the needle. Missing one of them can make a big difference in the quality of your stitches.

 Set the thread spool on the spindle.

A. Vertical spindle: Position the spool so that it will turn clockwise as you sew.

B. Horizontal spindle. The spool is held in place with an end cap. If your spool has a small cut in one end for minding the thread, position the spool with that end to the right.

TIP: If the spool is new and has paper labels covering the holes, poke them in, completely uncovering the holes, to allow the spool to turn freely.

Unless your machine has a self-winding bobbin, you will want to wind the bobbin before threading the machine (page 13).

 Pull thread to the left and through the first thread guide.

 Draw thread through the tension guide.

TIP: It is very important to have the presser foot lever up when threading the machine, because the tension discs are then open. If the presser foot is down and the discs are closed, the thread will not slide between the discs, and your stitches will not make you happy.

 Draw thread through the next thread guide.

 Insert thread through the take-up lever.

 Draw the thread through the remaining thread guides.

 Thread the needle. Most needles are threaded from front to back; some, from left to right.

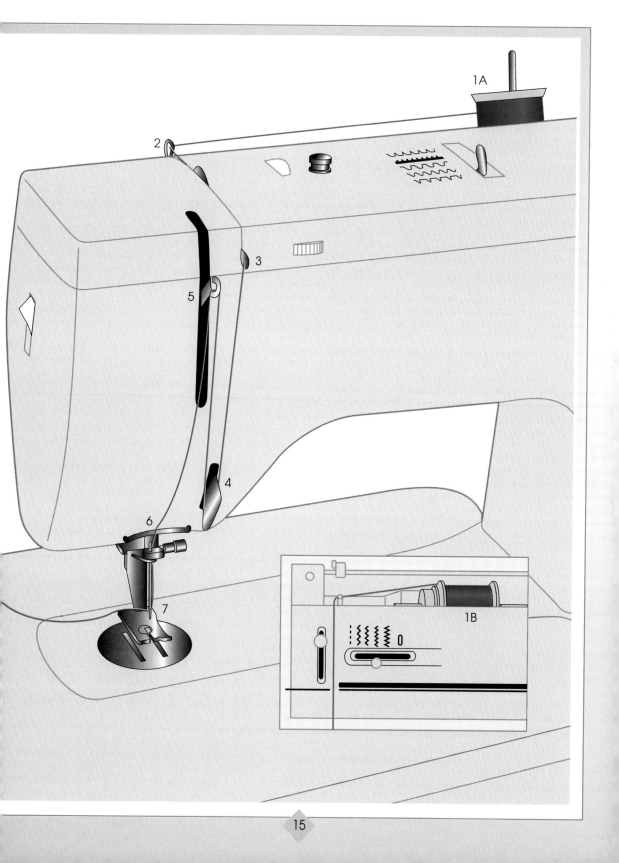

How to
Balance Tension

Your machine forms stitches by interlocking the bobbin thread with the needle thread. Every time the needle goes down into the fabric, a sharp hook catches the needle thread and wraps the bobbin thread around it. Imagine this little tug-of-war. If the needle thread tension is "stronger" than the bobbin thread tension, the needle thread pulls the bobbin thread through to the top. If the bobbin thread tension is "stronger," it pulls the needle thread through to the bottom. When the tensions are evenly balanced, the stitch will lock exactly halfway between the top and bottom of the layers being sewn, which is right where you want it.

Some machines have "self-adjusting tension," meaning the machine automatically adjusts its tension with every fabric you sew. For machines that do not have this feature, you may have to adjust the needle thread tension slightly as you sew different fabrics.

Testing the Tension

1 Thread your machine and insert the bobbin, using two very different colors of thread, neither of which matches the fabric. Cut an 8" (20.5 cm) square of a smooth, mediumweight fabric. Fold the fabric in half diagonally, and place it under the presser foot so the fold aligns to your 1/2" (1.3 cm) seam guide. Lower the presser foot and set your stitch length at 10 stitches per inch or 2.5 mm long.

Stitch a line across the fabric, stitching 1/2" (1.3 cm) from the diagonal fold. Remove the fabric from the machine. Inspect your stitching line from both sides. If your tension is evenly balanced, you will see only one color on each side. If you see both thread colors on the top side of your sample, the needle tension is tighter than the bobbin tension. If you see both thread colors on the back side of your sample, the bobbin tension is tighter than the needle tension.

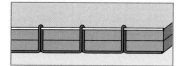
Top tension too tight

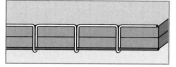
Top tension too loose

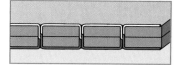
Tensions even

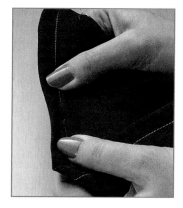

Adjusting the Tension

Before adjusting the tension on your machine, first check:
- that your machine is properly threaded (page 14)
- that your bobbin is properly installed
- that your needle is not damaged and is inserted correctly

Pull on your stitching line until you hear threads break. (Because you stitched on the **BIAS**, the fabric will stretch slightly.) If the thread breaks on only one side, your machine's tension is tighter on that side.

After checking these three things, you may need to adjust the tension on your machine. (Check your owner's manual.) Tighten or loosen the needle thread tension *slightly* to bring the needle thread and bobbin thread tensions into balance. Test the stitches after each adjustment, until you achieve balanced tension. If slight adjustments of the needle tension dial do not solve the problem, the bobbin tension may need adjusting. However, most manufacturers do not recommend that you adjust bobbin tension yourself, so unless you have received instructions for your machine, take your machine to the repairman.

Sewing a *Seam*

You may or may not be familiar with the very basic technique of running your machine and sewing a seam. Use this exercise as a refresher course whenever you feel you have lost touch with the basics or if your personal technique has become sloppy. Little frustrations, such as thread jams, erratic stitching lines, or having the thread pull out of the needle at the start of a seam, can often be prevented or corrected by following these basic guidelines. If you are really not sure where to begin, then you should probably begin right here!

1 Thread your machine (page 14) and insert the bobbin (page 13). Holding the needle thread with your left hand, turn the handwheel toward you until the needle has gone down and come back up to its highest point. A stitch will form, and you will feel a tug on the needle thread. Pull on the needle thread to bring the bobbin thread up through the hole in the throat plate. Pull both threads together under the presser foot and off to one side.

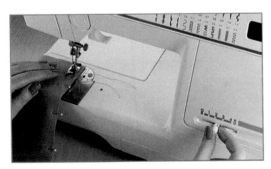

2 Cut rectangles of mediumweight fabric. Place the pieces right sides together, aligning the outer edges. Pin the pieces together along one long edge, inserting the pins about every 2" (5 cm), perpendicular to the edge. Place the fabric under the presser foot so the pinned side edges align to the 1/2" (1.3 cm) seam guide and the upper edges align to the back of the presser foot. Lower the presser foot, and set your stitch length at 2.5 mm, which equals 10 stitches per inch.

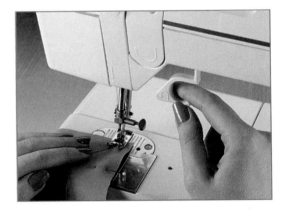

3 Begin by **backstitching** several stitches to the upper edge of the fabric. Hold the thread tails under a finger for the first few stitches. This prevents the needle thread from being pulled out of the needle and also prevents the thread tails from being drawn down into the bobbin case, where they could potentially cause the dreaded **thread jam**.

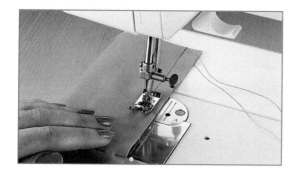

4 Stitch forward over the backstitched line, and continue sewing the ½" (1.3 cm) seam. Gently guide the fabric while you sew by walking your fingers ahead of and slightly to the sides of the presser foot. Remember, you are only guiding; let the machine pull the fabric.

Backstitching secures the beginning and end of your stitching line so that the stitches will not pull out. The method for backstitching varies with each sewing machine. You may need to lift and hold your stitch length lever, push in and hold a button, or simply touch an icon. Check your owner's manual.

Thread jams. No matter how conscientious you are at trying to prevent them, thread jams just seem to be lurking out there waiting to mess up your day. DON'T USE FORCE! Remove the presser foot, if you can. Snip all the threads you can get at from the top of the throat plate. Open the bobbin case door or throat plate, and snip any threads you can get at. Remove the bobbin, if you can. Gently remove the fabric. Thoroughly clean out the feed dog and bobbin area before reinserting the bobbin and starting over. Then just chalk it up to experience and get over it!

5 Stop stitching and remove pins as you come to them. When you reach the end of the fabric, stop stitching; backstitch several stitches, and stop again. Turn the handwheel toward you until the needle is in its highest position.

TIP: Straight stitching lines are easier to achieve if you watch the edge of the fabric along the seam guide and ignore the needle. Sew smoothly at a relaxing pace, with minimal starting and stopping, and without bursts of speed. You have better control of the speed if you operate your foot control with your heel resting on the floor.

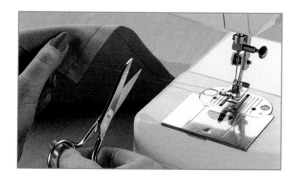

6 Raise the presser foot. Pull the fabric smoothly away from the presser foot, either to the left side or straight back. If you have to tug the threads, turn your handwheel slightly toward you until they pull easily. Cut the threads, leaving tails 2½" to 3" (6.5 to 7.5 cm) long.

Sewing Supplies

The sewing process for making nursery decor involves five basic steps: measuring, marking, cutting, stitching, and pressing. For each of these steps there are special tools and supplies to make your sewing easier and enhance your chances of completing a project successfully. You may already own some of these tools and supplies, but don't feel that you must get all of them before you start sewing. You will probably need more than one cutting tool, for instance, but you don't need them all, and you will undoubtedly acquire tools as your skills and interest grow.

Hand-sewing Supplies

Needles and pins are available in a variety of sizes and styles. Look for rustproof needles and pins made of brass, nickel-plated steel, or stainless steel. Pictured from top to bottom:

Sharps are all-purpose, medium-length needles designed for general sewing.

Crewels are sharp, large-eyed medium-length needles, designed for embroidery.

Betweens are very short and round-eyed. They are useful for hand quilting and making fine stitches.

Milliner's needles are long with round eyes and are used for making long basting or gathering stitches.

Straight pins are used for general sewing. They should be slim and are usually 1¹/₁₆" (2.7 cm) long. Pins with colored ball heads are easier to see and are less likely to get lost than those with flat heads.

Quilting pins are 1³/₄" (4.5 cm) long. Their extra length makes them ideal for use on bulky fabrics or fabrics with extra loft.

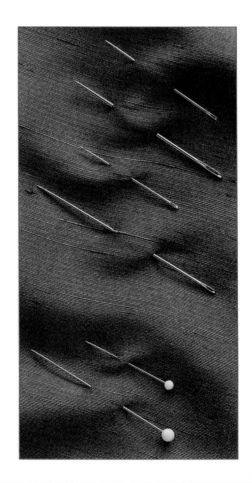

A Thimble protects your finger while hand sewing. Available in a variety of styles and sizes, it is worn on whichever finger you use to push the needle through the fabric. Most people prefer either the middle or ring finger. Using a thimble is an acquired habit. Some people can't get along without it, while others can never get used to it.

B Pincushion provides a safe and handy place to store pins. One style is worn on the wrist for convenience. Another style, a magnetic tray, attracts and holds steel pins. Be careful not to place any magnetic tools near a computerized machine, because the magnet may interfere with the machine's memory.

C Needle threader eases threading of hand and machine needles. This is especially useful if you have difficulty seeing something that small.

D Beeswax with holder strengthens thread and prevents tangling while hand sewing.

Measuring & Marking Tools

A Transparent ruler allows you to see what you are measuring and marking. It also is used to check fabric grainline.

B Yardstick (meterstick) should be made of smooth hardwood or metal.

C Tape measure has the flexibility helpful for measuring items with shape and dimension. Select one made of a material that will not stretch.

D Seam gauge is a 6" (15 cm) metal or plastic ruler with a sliding marker. It helps make quick, accurate measurements and can be used to measure seam allowance widths.

E Transparent T-square is used to locate grainlines and to measure 90° angles.

F Marking chalk is available in several forms; as powder in a rolling wheel dispenser, as a pencil, or as a flat slice. Chalk lines are easily removable from most fabrics.

G Fabric marking pens are available in both air-erasable and water-erasable forms. Air-erasable marks disappear in 48 hours; water-erasable marks wash off with a sprinkling of water.

H Narrow masking tape is an alternative method for marking fabrics when other methods are less suitable.

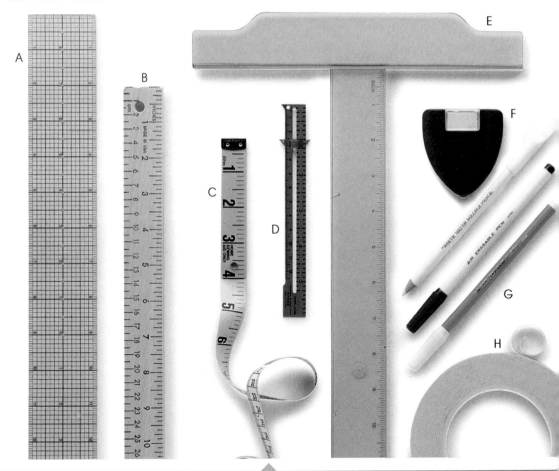

Cutting Tools

Buy quality cutting tools and use them only for your sewing! Cutting paper or other household materials will dull your cutting tools quickly. Dull tools are not only tiresome to work with, they can also damage fabric. Scissors have both handles the same size; shears have one handle larger than the other. The best-quality scissors and shears are hot-forged, high-grade steel, honed to a fine cutting edge. Blades should be joined with an adjustable screw to ensure even pressure along the length of the blade. Have your cutting tools sharpened periodically by a qualified professional.

I Bent-handled dressmaker's shears are best for cutting fabric shapes because the angle of the lower blade lets fabric lie flat on the cutting surface. Blade lengths of 7" or 8" (18 or 20.5 cm) are most popular, but lengths of up to 12" (30.5 cm) are available. Select a blade length appropriate for the size of your hand; shorter lengths for smaller hands. Left-handed models are also available. If you intend to sew a great deal, invest in a pair of all-steel, chrome-plated shears for heavy-duty cutting. Lighter models with stainless steel blades and plastic handles are fine for less-frequent sewing or light-weight fabrics.

J Sewing scissors have one pointed and one rounded tip for clipping threads and trimming and clipping seam allowances. A 6" (15 cm) blade is suitable for most tasks.

K Seam ripper quickly removes stitches and opens buttonholes. Use it carefully to avoid cutting the fabric.

L Rotary cutter works like a pizza cutter and can be used by left-handed or right-handed sewers. A locking mechanism retracts the blade for safety. Use the rotary cutter with a special plastic mat available in different sizes, with or without grid lines. The self-healing mat protects both the work surface and the blade.

M Pinking shears and pinking rotary cutters are used to finish seams. They cut fabric in a zigzag or scalloped pattern instead of a straight line.

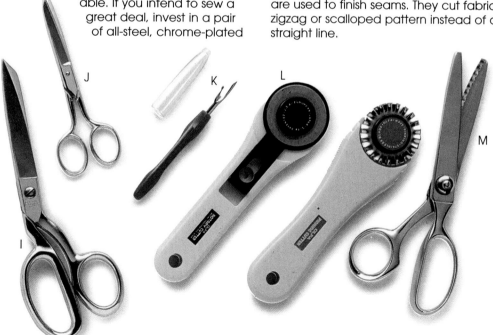

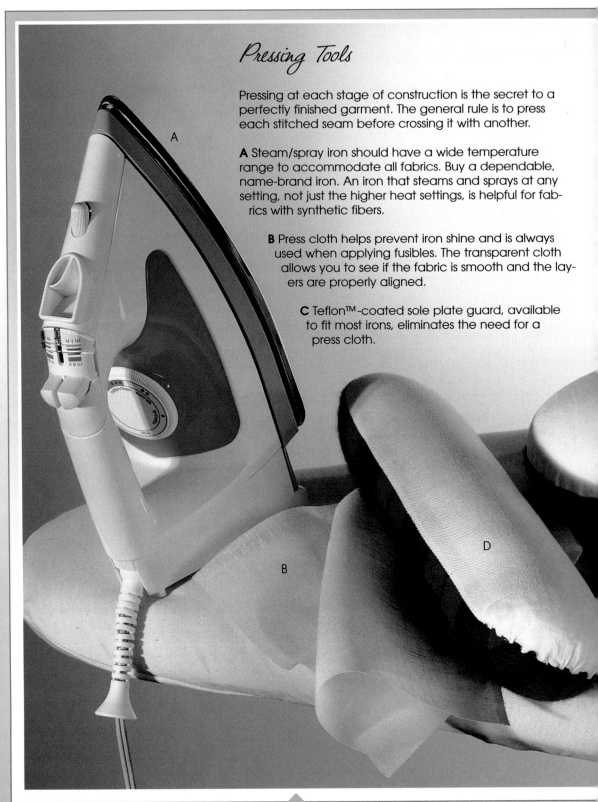

Pressing Tools

Pressing at each stage of construction is the secret to a perfectly finished garment. The general rule is to press each stitched seam before crossing it with another.

A Steam/spray iron should have a wide temperature range to accommodate all fabrics. Buy a dependable, name-brand iron. An iron that steams and sprays at any setting, not just the higher heat settings, is helpful for fabrics with synthetic fibers.

B Press cloth helps prevent iron shine and is always used when applying fusibles. The transparent cloth allows you to see if the fabric is smooth and the layers are properly aligned.

C Teflon™-coated sole plate guard, available to fit most irons, eliminates the need for a press cloth.

D Seam roll is a firmly packed cylindrical cushion for pressing seams. The bulk of the fabric falls to the sides away from the iron, preventing the seam from making an imprint on the right side of the fabric.

E Pressing ham is a firmly packed cushion for pressing curved areas of a garment.

F Sleeve board looks like two small ironing boards attached one on top of the other. It is useful for pressing sleeves one layer at a time to avoid unwanted creases.

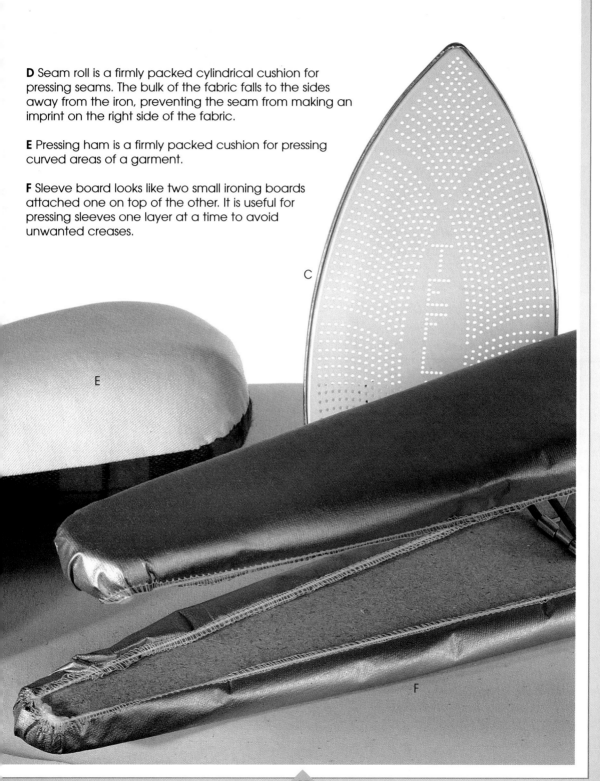

Special Products

Many special products and gadgets are designed for various steps of the sewing process. Just as you invest in and stock up on products for other aspects of your life, consider and buy these aids according to your sewing needs. The more you sew, the more these products will become a necessity.

Before using a new product, read any instructions carefully. Learn what special handling or care is required, and for what fabrics or techniques it is suited. Here are some specialized products, available in fabric stores, that you may find helpful in sewing nursery decor items.

Blanket binding resembles a wide satin ribbon that has been pressed in half for encasing the raw edge around a blanket. Packaged in a convenient length for sewing baby blankets, the binding is available in assorted soft colors and white. Because of its stability and permanent crease, it is easy to work with, yet feels silky smooth against your baby's skin.

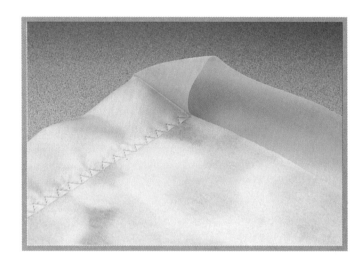

Double-fold bias tape is a convenient item, useful for countless sewing situations where raw edges must be encased for a durable and decorative finish. The manufacturer has already cut the bias strips, sewn them together, and pressed in precise folds to make your sewing easier. The tapes, in both regular and extra-wide widths, are available in packaged lengths in a wide range of colors.

Bodkin is used to thread elastic through a casing, as for the crib sheet. One end holds the elastic tightly while you feed the tool through the narrow casing.

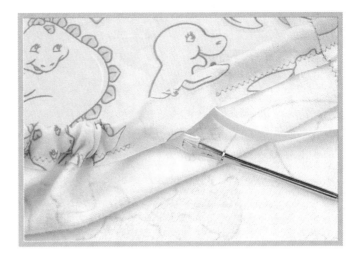

Buttonhole cutter is a handy tool for making precision cuts down the center of buttonholes. It comes with a wooden block to place under the fabric, to protect your work surface and accept the sharp thin blade of the cutter. While buttonholes can be cut open with small scissors or a seam ripper, a buttonhole cutter is more accurate and less likely to cut the stitches.

Point turner is helpful for perfecting corners, such as for lined-to-the-edge window toppers, pillows, or padded wall shapes. Made of wood or plastic, its point neatly fits into corners without tearing the fabric.

continued

Special Products (continued)

Glue stick is a convenient substitute for pinning or basting when you need to hold an item in place temporarily before stitching.

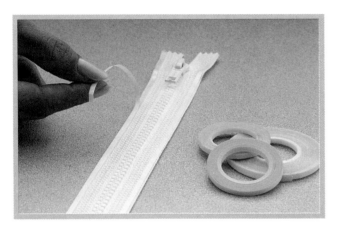

Basting tape is double-faced adhesive tape used instead of pinning or hand basting for temporarily securing items to be stitched. It is especially helpful for applying zippers and trims. Position the tape so that the needle will not stitch through it because the adhesive may collect on your machine needle.

Liquid fray preventer is a colorless plastic liquid that prevents fraying by stiffening the fabric slightly. It is helpful when you have clipped too far into a seam allowance or want to reinforce a buttonhole. It may darken some colors, so test before using and apply carefully. The liquid may be removed with rubbing alcohol. It dries to a permanent finish that will withstand laundering and dry cleaning.

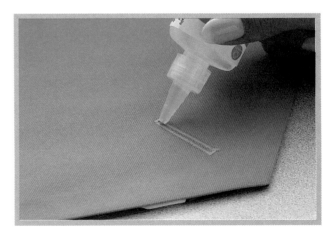

Fusible interfacing plays a supporting role in many sewn items. It can be purchased by the yard (meter) or in packaged amounts. Most often it is used in garments to stabilize areas around necklines or behind buttons. You will also find it handy for closing the slit openings on the backs of padded wall shapes.

Paper-backed fusible web is available on rolls, in various narrow widths, or rolled on a bolt for purchase by the yard (meter). It is a timesaving product used for adhering two pieces of fabric together. For instance, you may use a narrow strip of it to close an opening along the side of a window topper. Or you may use the wider form to apply appliqués to the surface of padded wall shapes. A protective paper backing is removed from one side after the other side has been fused to fabric.

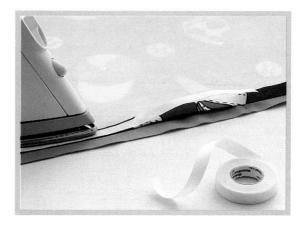

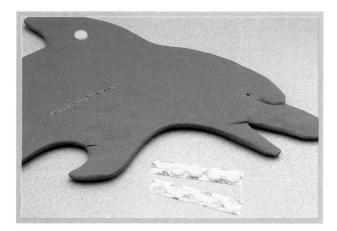

Velcro® dots have an adhesive backing for securing two things together without the hassle of hand or machine stitching. Use them to mount padded wall shapes by adhering the hook side to the wall and the loop side (the softer side) to the wall shape.

Fabric Information

Choosing the fabrics for your nursery decorating projects can be a lot of fun, if you arm yourself with a few fabric facts and a thought-through plan. While the fabric suggestions for each project will help you narrow the field, there are oceans of possibilities out there. It will be helpful to learn as much as you can about fabrics by reading this section. Then browse through a fabric store, handling the fabrics and reading the fiber content and care information printed on the ends of the bolts.

You probably want coordinating prints and solid color fabrics for the various projects you intend to sew. Be sure to consider the ease of care, as many items in a nursery are laundered often.

Types of Fabrics

Natural fabrics are made from plant or animal fibers, spun into yarns; cotton, wool, silk, and linen are the most common. Naturals are often considered the easiest fabrics to sew. Chemically produced synthetic fabrics are made to resemble the look and feel of natural fabrics. Polyester may look like cotton or silk, acetate and nylon shimmer like silk, and acrylic mimics the texture and appearance of wool. Rayon is a man-made fiber from a plant source. Each fiber has unique characteristics, desirable for different reasons. Many fabrics are a blend of natural and synthetic fibers, offering you the best qualities of each, such as the soft comfort of cotton blended with the wrinkle resistance of polyester.

More About
Fabric

Woven Fabrics

Woven fabrics have straight lengthwise and crosswise yarns. The pattern in which the yarns are woven gives the fabric its characteristic surface texture and appearance. The outer edges of woven fabrics are called **SELVAGES.** As a general rule, they should be trimmed away because they are often denser than the rest of the fabric, and they may shrink when laundered or pressed. Grainlines are the directions in which the fabric yarns run. Strong, stable lengthwise yarns, running parallel to the selvages, form the **LENGTHWISE GRAIN.** The **CROSSWISE GRAIN** is perpendicular to the lengthwise grain and has a small amount of give. Any diagonal direction, called the **BIAS,** has a fair amount of stretch.

Woven fabrics suitable for nursery decor include plain weaves in various weights, **(A),** twills, such as lightweight denim **(B),** satin weaves, which have a natural sheen **(C),** fine-wale corduroy **(D),** and flannel **(E),** all of which are available in prints and solid colors.

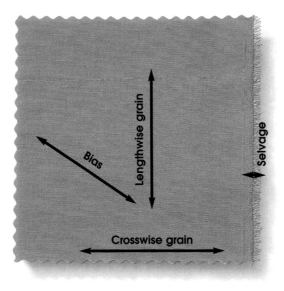

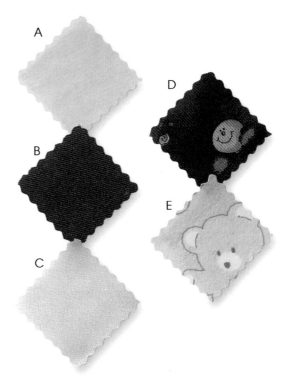

Knit Fabrics

Knit fabrics consist of rows of interlocking loops of yarn, similar to a hand-knit sweater, but on a finer scale. Knit fabrics are more flexible than other fabrics, and they stretch, making them less desirable for items like crib skirts or diaper stackers. Fine cotton or cotton/polyester knits **(A)** are suitable for crib sheets, however. Robe velour **(B)** and sweatshirt fleece **(C)** are knits with very little stretch and are suitable for bumper pads. Synthetic fleece **(D)**, which is a reversible knit fabric, is an excellent choice for cozy blankets.

A

B

C

D

Prequilted Fabrics

Prequilted fabrics consist of a layer of batting sandwiched between two fabrics. The layers are held in place by a network of stitching lines. They are often reversible, making them suitable for baby blankets. Single-sided quilted fabrics can be used for nap-time totes or to make wall shapes with extra padding.

Even More About *Fabric*

Shopping

Fabrics in a store are divided into *fashion fabrics* and *decorator fabrics*. Decorator fabrics, designed for pillows, slipcovers, window treatments, and other home decorating projects, are generally more durable than fashion fabrics; most have stain-resistant finishes. For this reason, it is often recommended that decorator fabrics be dry-cleaned rather than laundered, which could be a drawback for some nursery items. One advantage of decorator fabrics is that they are often manufactured in coordinating groups so you can mix and match fabrics for a foolproof scheme. They are manufactured in widths (crosswise grain) of 48" or 54" (122 or 137 cm), though occasionally you may find some wider. To prevent creases, decorator fabrics are rolled on tubes in a single layer.

Fashion fabrics are usually folded double and rolled on cardboard bolts. They vary in width; the most common are 36", 45", and 60" (91.5, 115, and 152.5 cm). Though fashion fabrics are intended for apparel, many of them are also suitable for nursery decor

items. Most stores arrange their fashion fabrics according to the fiber content or fabric style. For instance, all the cottons suitable for quilting projects might be located in one area; bridal and special occasion fabrics in another. You will also find coordinating prints and solids.

Fabric Preparation

Every bolt or tube of fabric should carry a fabric identification label, which tells you its fiber content, width, and care method;

information that is essential to your selection. Preshrink washable fabrics before cutting out the pieces, by washing and drying them in the same way you will care for the finished items. Because most decorator fabrics are not washable and require dry cleaning, preshrink them by pressing with steam, moving the iron evenly along the grainlines. Allow the fabric to dry completely before moving it.

Hand Stitches

While modern sewers rely on sewing machines for speedy construction, there are situations when hand stitching is necessary or preferable. You may need to slipstitch an opening closed in a pillow, or hand-baste a decorative trim in place until you sew it permanently by machine. And, of course, the art of sewing on buttons is a valuable skill for anyone to master.

Threading the Needle

Insert the thread end through the needle's eye, for sewing with a single strand. Or fold the thread in half, and insert the fold through the eye, for sewing with a double strand. Pull through about 8" (20.5 cm). Wrap the other end(s) around your index finger. Then, using your thumb, roll the thread off your finger, twisting it into a knot.

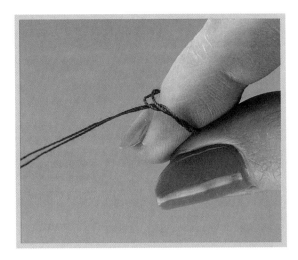

TIP: Use a single strand when slipstitching or basting. Use a double strand when sewing on buttons. To avoid tangles, begin with thread no longer than 18" (46 cm) from the needle to the knot. Run the thread though beeswax (page 21), if desired.

Basting

Thread a long needle with a single white or contrasting thread; knot the end. Enter the fabric from the top and come up about 1" (2.5 cm) away, catching all layers in the stitch. Pull the stitch snug, but not tight, so the layers lie flat and will not shift. Continue taking 1" (2.5 cm) stitches until you have reached the end of your basting line. Take a short stitch backward, over the last stitch, to secure the thread temporarily. Clip the thread, leaving a short tail.

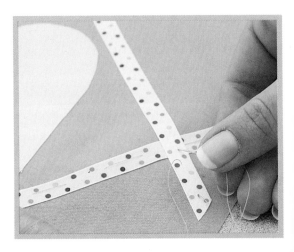

Slipstitching

1 Insert the threaded needle under the seam allowance, just behind the opening. Bring it to the outside in the seamline. If you are right-handed, work from right to left; lefties work from left to right.

2 Insert the needle into the fold just behind where the thread came up, and run it inside the fold for about 1/4" (6 mm). Bring the needle out, and draw the thread snug. Take your next stitch in the opposite fold, inserting the needle directly across from the previous stitch.

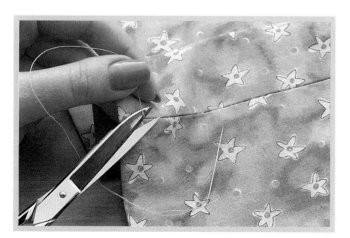

3 Continue, crossing from one fold to the other, until you have sewn past the opening. Secure the thread with several tiny stitches in the seamline. Then take a long stitch, and pull it tight. Clip the thread at the fabric surface, and let the tail disappear inside.

Sewing on a Shank Button

1 Place the button on the mark, with the shank hole parallel to the buttonhole. Secure the thread on the right side of the fabric with a small stitch under the button.

2 Bring the needle through the shank hole. Insert the needle down through the fabric and pull the thread through. Take four to six stitches in this manner.

3 Secure the thread in the fabric under the button by making a knot or taking several small stitches. Clip the thread ends.

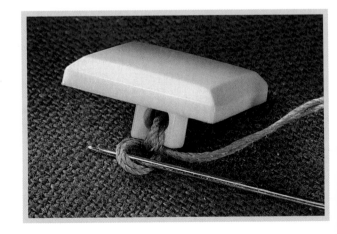

Sewing on a Sew-through Button

1 Place the button on the mark, with the holes lining up parallel to the buttonhole. Bring the needle through the fabric from the underside and up through one hole in the button. Insert the needle into another hole and though the fabric layers.

2 Slip a toothpick, match, or sewing machine needle between the thread and the button to form a shank. Take three or four stitches through each pair of holes. Bring the needle and thread to the right side under the button. Remove the toothpick.

3 Wind the thread two or three times around the button stitches to form the shank. Secure the thread on the right side under the button, by making a knot or taking several small stitches. Clip the threads close to the knot.

Baby Blanket

Blankets serve many purposes in the day-to-day routine of baby care. Most often they provide comfort, warmth, and security for little tykes. A blanket also provides a soft surface for rolling around on the floor or a make-do pad for a quick change when you're on the go. With easy-to-apply blanket binding and synthetic fleece fabric, you can sew up new blankets in a jiffy. Because the following method involves the use of fabric glue, you'll want to launder the finished blanket before you use it.

WHAT YOU'LL LEARN

How to apply satin blanket binding

The secret to sewing **MITERED** corners

The importance of careful **PRESSING**

WHAT YOU'LL NEED

1 yd. (0.95 m) synthetic fleece

Satin blanket binding in color to match or coordinate with fabric

Quilting ruler or carpenter's square

Fabric glue stick

Thread to match blanket binding

Let's Begin

1 Cut a rectangle of fabric 36" x 45" (91.5 x 115 cm). Use a quilter's ruler or carpenter's square to ensure square corners. In the following steps, unroll the binding from the package as you need it, and don't cut it until step 7.

TIP: Synthetic fleece is actually a knit fabric and is usually 60" (152.5 cm) wide. Avoid using either of the **SELVAGES** as a side of your rectangle because they may be slightly stretched out of shape.

2 Beginning about 10" (25.5 cm) from one corner and working toward the corner in a clockwise direction, slip the blanket edge between the layers of the binding. Tuck the edge in as close as possible to the binding fold. Insert pins through all the layers, perpendicular to the edge. Space the pins about 2" (5 cm) apart with the heads outward.

TIP: Be sure to keep the binding folded smooth and flat over the edge, so that the outer crease remains sharp. This will ensure that the finished binding edges on the front and back of the blanket are perfectly aligned.

3 Set the machine to a **MULTISTITCH-ZIGZAG** at maximum width and 12 stitches per inch, which equals 2 mm. Place the blanket under the presser foot at the binding end, with the inner edge of the binding aligned to the *left side of the presser foot opening.* Stitch to the fabric edge, removing pins as you come to them. Stop, and *remove the fabric from the machine.*

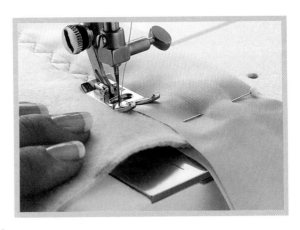

Take the blanket to the ironing board.
Open out the binding at the corner,
and fold it down along the next side, so
that the fabric edge aligns to the binding
fold. A 45° angle will form in the binding.
PRESS the angle lightly with the tip of the iron.

Left side of the presser foot opening.
The opening in the center of the presser foot is more than wide enough to
accommodate the widest stitch your
machine can sew. Guide the fabric,
keeping a tiny space between the
binding edge and the left edge of the
opening. The farthest left stitch of the
needle should just stitch off the edge
of the binding. Adjust the position
slightly, if necessary.

Remove the fabric from the machine.
When you finish a stitching line, always
stop with the needle out of the fabric
and the take-up lever in the highest
position. (Some newer machines
automatically do this for you.) Raise
the presser foot; pull the fabric to the
side or toward the back. Clip the
threads, leaving several inches (centimeters) of thread extending from the
needle and bobbin.

Fold the binding
closed so that the
angled fold forms
a **MITERED** corner. The
fold runs diagonally from
the outer corner to the
inner corner, matching
up perfectly.

continued

continued

6 Flip the blanket over and miter the back of the binding so that the diagonal fold on the back also lines up perfectly. Using a fabric glue stick, secure the folds in place. This is called *glue-basting.*

7 Encase and pin the blanket edge to the next corner. Place the blanket under the presser foot, aligning the inner corner of the miter to the left side of the presser foot opening. *Backstitch (pg. 19)* two or three stitches. Stitch forward to the fabric edge at the next corner. Stop, and remove the blanket from the machine.

8 Repeat steps 4 to 7 for the remaining corners. On the side where you started, cut the binding 4" (10 cm) beyond the beginning. Open the fold; press under 2" (5 cm) at the end.

Glue-basting. Use a fabric glue stick. This versatile product may become one of your favorite sewing tools. The temporary adhesive in a handy retractable tube can be applied in small dabs or continuous lines. It won't discolor the fabric and will wash out completely, if necessary.

Reset the stitch length to 0. The machine will still stitch side to side, as it is still set for multistitch-zigzag, but the fabric will not move forward.

9 Refold and finish encasing and pinning the blanket edge. The folded end should overlap the cut end 2" (5 cm). Glue-baste the folded end in place. Stitch the last side, stitching about 1" (2.5 cm) beyond the over-lap. Remove the blanket from the machine, and clip the threads.

10 **Reset the stitch length to 0.** Place the overlapped bind-ing ends under the press-er foot so that the fold is about 1/4" (6 mm) ahead of the presser foot opening. Stitch in place until the needle has traveled from left to right at least twice. This **TACKING** will keep the ends in place through many launderings.

Now that was pretty easy!

Preliminary steps that include pinning, pressing, and glue-basting may seem tedious but they make a world of difference in the ease and precision of the final stitching.

Fitted Sheets

Standard crib sheets are available ready-made in a variety of colors and prints, so the idea of making your own sheets might not appeal to you. But if you plan on sewing a bumper pad and skirt for your crib, you may also want to sew sheets in coordinating colors. Or, if you have a bassinette or cradle, chances are you cannot find sheets to fit. For baby's comfort, sew the sheets from soft cotton knit fabric. Be sure to **PRESHRINK** the fabric because cotton knit fabric will shrink substantially.

Two methods are shown; one for mattresses with square corners and the other for rounded corners. Both involve sewing a **CASING** to hold elastic for a snug fit.

WHAT YOU'LL LEARN

Tricks for sewing on knit fabrics

Two methods for sewing a casing

How to press-shape bias tape to fit a curve

WHAT YOU'LL NEED

Cotton knit fabric, 60" (152.5 cm) wide: 2¼ yd. (2.1 m) for standard crib mattress; see cutting directions for nonstandard sizes

Extra wide double-fold bias tape, for round corner method

⅜" (1 cm) elastic: 2½ yd. (2.3 m) for standard mattress; see directions for nonstandard sizes

Thread to match the fabric

Let's Begin

1. ***Preshrink the fabric.*** Cut a rectangle 68" x 43" (173 x 109 cm), with the longer direction following the **LENGTHWISE GRAIN,** which is the least stretchy direction of the fabric. Cut an 8½" (21.8 cm) square from each corner of the rectangle; discard the squares.

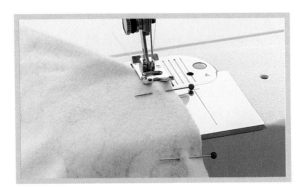

2. Fold the sheet, right sides together, at one corner, matching the two 8½" (21.8 cm) edges. Pin the edges together, inserting the pins perpendicular to the edges. Set the sewing machine for a narrow, short **ZIGZAG** stitch or **STRETCH STITCH.** Check your owner's manual for directions. Place the pinned edges under the presser foot, aligning the raw edges to a *¼" (6 mm) seam allowance guide.*

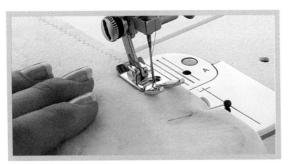

3. Stitch the **SEAM,** *backstitching (p. 19)* at the beginning and end. Stitch the seams in the remaining three corners the same way. **PRESS** all of the **SEAM ALLOWANCES** to one side, all in the same direction.

TIP: You will find it much easier to insert the elastic into the casing if all of the seam allowances are pressed in the same direction. The bodkin can then pass easily over them.

4. Turn under and press ¾" (2 cm) all around the sheet; pin. Set the machine for a narrow zigzag. Beginning anywhere, place the fabric under the presser foot with the bulk of the sheet to the left of the needle and the folded edge aligned to the ⅝" (1.5 cm) seam allowance guide. Stitch, forming the casing. ***Remove the pins as you come to them.*** Backstitch at the beginning and end, leaving a 2" (5 cm) opening.

5 Fasten a bodkin or safety pin to one end of the elastic, and insert it through the casing opening, aiming it in the same direction in which the seam allowances are pressed. Push and pull the bodkin through the casing to the opposite side of the opening.

TIP: Insert a large safety pin across the free end of the elastic so that it will not get pulled into the opening.

6 Check to see that the elastic is not twisted inside the casing. Pull the ends of the elastic several inches (centimeters) out of the casing; overlap them ½" (1.3 cm). Place them under the presser foot, and stitch through both layers, using a short, wide **MULTISTITCH-ZIGZAG**.

7 Ease the elastic back into the casing. Stitch the opening closed, using the same stitch settings as for the rest of the casing. Distribute the casing **FULLNESS** evenly around the elastic.

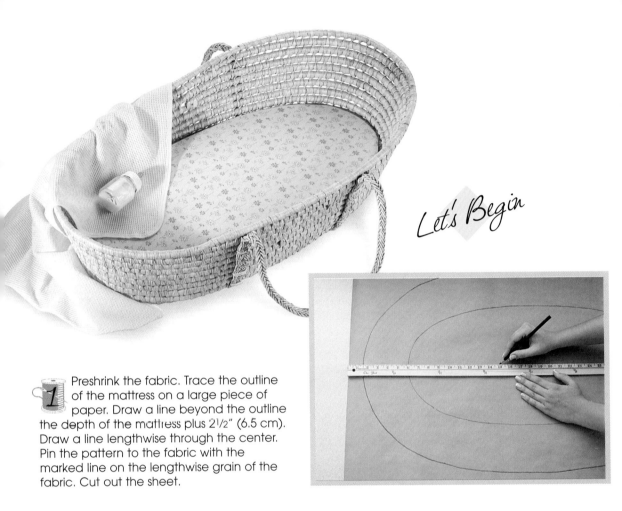

Let's Begin

1 Preshrink the fabric. Trace the outline of the mattress on a large piece of paper. Draw a line beyond the outline the depth of the mattress plus 2½" (6.5 cm). Draw a line lengthwise through the center. Pin the pattern to the fabric with the marked line on the lengthwise grain of the fabric. Cut out the sheet.

2 Unroll the double-fold bias tape and press it lightly to remove any wrinkles. Notice that one fold is shorter than the other. Place the sheet, right side up, on the iron-ing board. Starting on a fairly straight side, slip the sheet edge between the folds of the bias tape, with the **shorter fold on top.** Align the cut edge of the sheet to the inner crease of the tape. Pin.

Continue encasing the sheet edge inside the tape. In curved areas, shape the tape to fit the curve, and press with the iron, so it fits the edge smoothly, before pinning. When you complete the circle, cut the tape so that the ends just meet.

Quick Reference

Shorter fold on top. This will ensure that your stitches will also catch the slightly wider fold that is underneath. How clever and helpful of the bias tape manufacturer!

TIP: You could turn under the ends, but they are cut on the **BIAS** and will not fray. Plus, they will be hidden under the mattress. If one package is not enough, add more bias tape in the same way.

Set the machine for a narrow zigzag. Place the encased edge under the presser foot so that the needle will stitch close to the inner fold of the bias tape. Stitch all around the casing, overlapping the stitches where you begin and end. Remove pins as you come to them.

Cut elastic 15" (38 cm) shorter than the circumference of the mattress. Insert the elastic into the bias tape casing as in steps 5 and 6 on page 49. Ease the elastic back into the casing, and distribute the casing fullness evenly around the elastic.

Your sheet is complete,

and custom-made to fit the size and shape of your mattress. With elastic all around, it will fit smoothly and stay snugly tucked under.

Crib
Skirt

Dress up the crib and hide the metal springs and mattress support bars by sewing a softly gathered crib skirt. Unlike three-sided skirts designed for beds, this skirt surrounds all four sides of the crib, with a split at each corner to fit over the frame. The sides and end panels are sewn to a flat deck that rests on top of the crib springs. Select fabric to coordinate with a bumper pad, preferably one that is a solid color or that has a **NONDIRECTIONAL PRINT** so it can be **RAILROADED.** The fabric will be turned so that the **LENGTHWISE GRAIN** runs horizontally around the crib, eliminating the need for seams. Choose inexpensive plain **MUSLIN** or even an old sheet for the deck fabric.

WHAT YOU'LL LEARN

How to sew double-fold hems

How to **GATHER** a longer piece of fabric to fit a shorter piece

Shopping for the fabric is half the fun!

What is railroading and why do it?

WHAT YOU'LL NEED

3½ yd. (3.2 m) of fabric that can be railroaded, at least 45" (115 cm) wide

1⅝ yd. (1.5 m) muslin or an old sheet, for the deck

Strong thin cord, such as dental floss or crochet cotton

Thread to match or blend with the fabric

Let's Begin

1 Straighten the cut ends of the fabric, making sure they are perfectly perpendicular to the **SELVAGES.** Then trim away the selvages evenly. Cut the fabric lengthwise into three equal long strips. Cut 18" (46 cm) off the ends of two of the strips, for the skirt sides (perhaps you can use these pieces in another project). Cut the remaining long strip in half for the skirt ends.

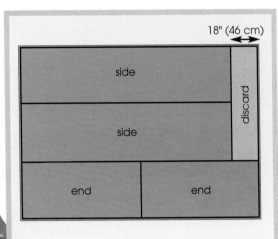

2 Press under 1" (2.5 cm) along the lower edge of one skirt section.

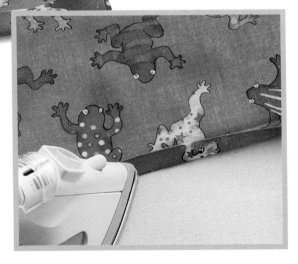

3 Unfold the pressed edge. Turn the cut edge back, aligning it to the first foldline; press the outer fold.

Press under. Place the fabric face-down on your ironing board. Fold the cut edge back; measure, and press, keeping the width of the folded edge consistent across the entire edge.

Double-fold hem. Side and bottom hems of many decorating items, like this crib skirt, are made with two folds of equal depth, encasing the cut edge in the crease of the outer fold. Pressing the first fold to the total hem depth, in this case 1" (2.5 cm), allows you to fold under and press the outer edge more accurately and easily.

4 Refold the edge along the pressed foldlines, encasing the raw edge to form a ¹/₂" (1.3 cm) **double-fold hem.** Pin the hem, inserting the pins perpendicular to the foldlines.

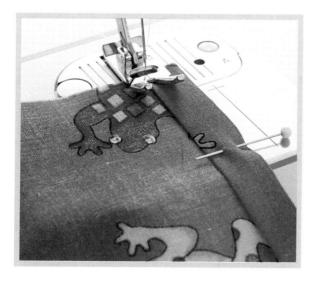

5 Place the pinned hem under the presser foot of the machine, with the wrong side of the skirt piece facing up. The bulk of the fabric is positioned to the left of the machine. The short cut end should align to the needle hole in the throat plate, with the needle aligned to enter the fabric just inside the inner fold.

continued

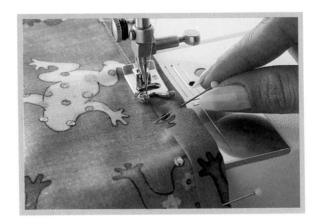

Stitch forward, guiding the fabric so that the needle stitches on the edge of the fold. Stop stitching and **remove pins as you come to them (p. 49).** Stitch the entire length of the hem, stopping with the needle up at the opposite cut edge. **Remove the fabric from the machine (p. 43).**

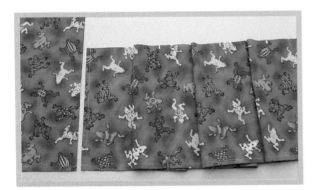

Repeat steps 2 to 6 for the bottom hems on the three remaining skirt pieces. Then hem the short ends in the same manner, but **backstitch (p. 19)** a few stitches at the beginning and end of the side hems. **MARK** each skirt piece along the upper edge, dividing the short pieces in half and the long pieces into quarters.

TIP: You will be joining the skirt to the deck with right sides together, so mark the fabric edges on the right side, using short lines perpendicular to the edge, within the ½" (1.3 cm) **SEAM ALLOWANCE.**

Cut a rectangle of muslin or old sheet for the deck that measures 1" (2.5 cm) longer and wider than the inside measurement of the crib frame. Mark a dot in each corner, ½" (1.3 cm) from the edges, using a light pencil or fabric marker. Mark the long sides between dots into quarters; mark the short sides in half.

9 Place the upper raw edge of one skirt panel under the presser foot of the machine, with the wrong side of the skirt piece facing up. The bulk of the fabric is positioned to the left of the machine. The short hemmed end should align to the opening in the presser foot and the cut edge should align to the 3/8" (1 cm) *seam allowance guide* on the bed of your machine. Unwind a length of strong cord, and place it under the center of the presser foot, allowing the end to extend several inches (centimeters) behind the foot. Lower the presser foot. Set the machine for a wide **ZIGZAG STITCH,** with medium length.

Quick Reference

Seam allowance guide. Most machines have a series of lines on the throat plate, just to the right of the presser foot. These lines mark the distance from the needle (when set to sew a standard straight-stitch seam) to the cut edges. Because sewing machines vary, measure the lines on your machine with the machine set on straight stitch and the needle down in the fabric. If your machine does not have a seam allowance guide, mark guide lines on the bed of the machine with tape.

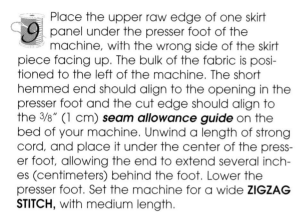

TIP: This technique may test your dexterity, but is easiest to accomplish if you guide the fabric with your left hand while allowing the cord to feed freely over the index finger of your right hand, held directly in front of the presser foot. Or, if you are fortunate enough to own a presser foot with a centered guide hole, feed the cord through the hole and guide the fabric with both hands.

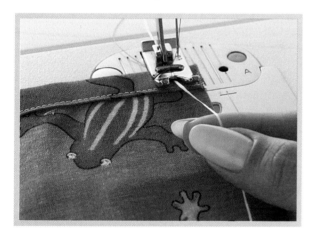

10 Stitch forward slowly, zigzagging over the cord, trapping it beneath the stitches but never piercing it. Continue across the entire upper edge. Leave a cord tail at the opposite end when you remove the fabric from the machine. Repeat this step at the top of each of the remaining three skirt pieces.

continued

continued

11 With right sides together, align the upper edge of one long skirt piece to a long edge of the deck, matching quarter marks. Align the hemmed ends to the dots, 1/2" (1.3 cm) from the corners. Insert pins from the skirt side, perpendicular to the edges at each set of marks. Pin the hemmed ends to the deck, 1/2" (1.3 cm) from the corners.

12 At one end, grasp the cord and pull on it, sliding the fabric along the cord to gather it. Keep pulling on the cord, gathering the fabric and distributing the gathers evenly between the pins from the end to the halfway mark. When the skirt fabric is gathered up to fit that half, secure the cord by winding it in a figure eight around the end pin.

13 Pull the cord from the other end to gather the remaining half; secure the cord. Distribute all the gathered fabric evenly along the deck edge, inserting pins frequently to hold the fabric in place.

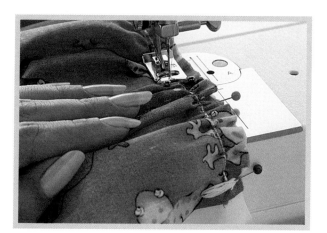

Finish the raw edges together. This will prevent the fabric from raveling when you launder the skirt. The skirt and deck edges can be finished together because they are both pressed toward the deck.

14 Reset the machine for a straight stitch with a length of 10 to 12 stitches per inch, which is 2 to 2.5 mm. Place the fabric under the presser foot, with the deck on the bottom and the raw edges aligned to the ½" (1.3 cm) seam allowance guide. Begin by backstitching at the end. Stitch forward, keeping the gathers even and removing the pins as you come to them. Finish by backstitching at the opposite end. Cut off excess cord.

15 Repeat steps 11 to 14 for each of the remaining skirt pieces. Reset the machine for a wide zigzag with a length of 10 to 12 stitches per inch (2 to 2.5 mm). **FINISH *the raw edges together*** all around the deck, stitching so that the right swing of the needle just clears the raw edges.

That's it!
Give the skirt a final pressing, and put it on the crib under the mattress.

Diaper Stacker

Keep diapers handy in this easy-to-sew, attractive diaper stacker. Made with convenient ties at the upper corners, the stacker can be secured to the crib rail or to knobs attached to the side of your changing table. A rectangle of foam-core board provides a firm, flat bottom for stacking an ample supply of disposable or cloth diapers. The front opening edges are enclosed in double-fold bias tape, a sewing notion that makes short work of binding raw edges, while adding a decorative touch.

WHAT YOU'LL LEARN

The importance of accuracy in measuring, cutting, and stitching

Using glue isn't necessarily cheating!

How to make a box corner

How to apply double-fold bias tape

WHAT YOU'LL NEED

7/8 yd. (0.8 m) fabric, 45" (115 cm) wide

Extra wide, double-fold bias tape, in a color to match or coordinate with the fabric

Thread to match the fabric and bias tape

Fabric glue stick

Quilting ruler or carpenter's square, for cutting perfect rectangles

8" x 12" (20.5 x 30.5 cm) rectangle of foam-core board

Let's Begin

1 Cut one rectangle of fabric 29" x 40"(73.5 x 102 cm), running the long sides along the **CROSSWISE GRAIN** of the fabric. Do not use a **SELVAGE** for a short side.

TIP: With the fabric folded in half lengthwise, measure and mark 29" (73.5 cm) along the fold. Then draw perpendicular lines 20" (51 cm) from the marks, and complete the rectangle, using a quilter's ruler or carpenter's square to ensure right angles. Cut out the rectangle through both layers at once.

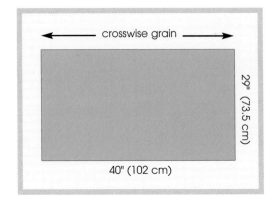

crosswise grain

29" (73.5 cm)

40" (102 cm)

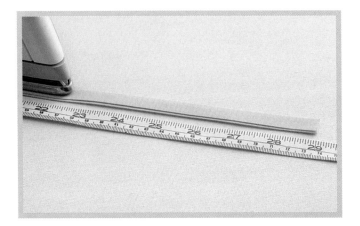

2 Unroll the double-fold bias tape and *press* it lightly to remove any wrinkles. Notice that one fold is shorter than the other. Cut off two strips, 29" (73.5 cm) long, and set them aside.

3 Set the machine for a straight stitch of 10 to 12 stitches per inch, which equals 2 to 2.5 mm. With the short fold on top and the center fold to the left, place one end of the remaining tape under the presser foot. The needle should be aligned to enter the short fold. Stitch the entire tape closed. Stitch slowly and accurately along the folded edge.

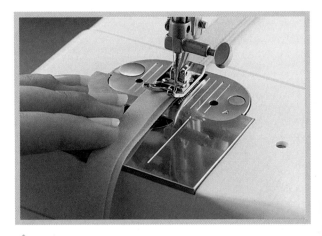

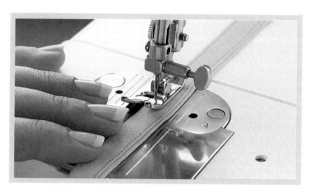

Quick Reference

Pressing. Use an up-and-down motion, lifting and lowering the iron in an over-lapping pattern. Avoid sliding the iron back and forth on the surface, as this may distort the shape, especially on a bias like this.

4 **Remove the tape from the machine (p. 43),** and place it under the presser foot so that the needle is aligned to enter the single fold on the opposite side. Stitch the entire length of the tape as near the fold as possible. This is called **EDGESTITCHING.** Cut the stitched tape in half, and set it aside for the ties.

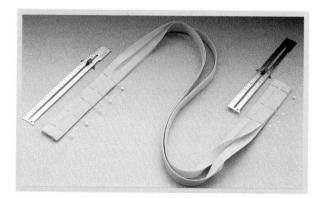

5 Open the 29" (73.5 cm) strips and pin them right sides together, 3" (7.5 cm) from the top end, matching the wide and narrow sides so that the center fold-lines are directly on top of each other. Mark a dot 3" (7.5 cm) from the end. Pin and mark the bottom ends in the same manner 4½" (11.5 cm) from the end.

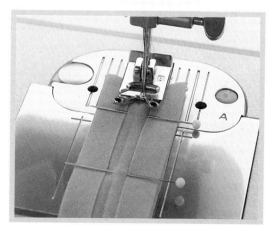

6 Place the tapes under the presser foot, aligning the tip of the needle to the center fold, about ¼" (6 mm) from the tape ends. Make sure the outer folds of the strips are still aligned.

continued

continued

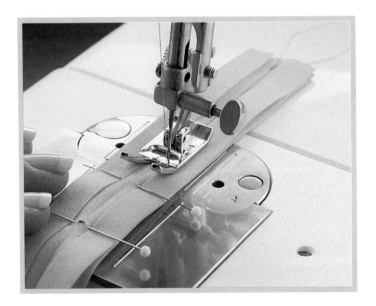

7 **Backstitch (p. 19)** two or three stitches; stop. Then, stitching forward, stitch down the center foldline up to the mark; **remove the pins (p. 49) as you come to them.** Backstitch two or three stitches, and remove the strips from the machine. Stitch the opposite ends together in the same manner.

8 Refold the joined strips with the **shorter folds on top (p. 51).** Slip one long edge of the fabric rectangle, right side up, between the folds of the left-hand strip, aligning the raw edge to the center fold. **Glue-baste (p. 45)** the bias tape strip over the fabric edge, matching up the ends of the strip to the upper and lower edges of the fabric.

TIP: Apply the glue to the inner folds of the bias tape, and then position the fabric between the folds and finger-press the tape closed. Small dabs of glue spaced about 1" (2.5 cm) apart should be sufficient.

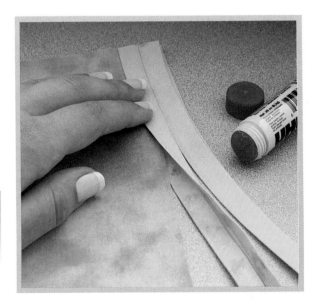

Place the encased edge under the presser foot, with the bulk of the fabric to the left of the machine and the needle aligned to enter the bias strip near the outer fold. Stitch slowly for accuracy. Because you are stitching with the narrower side of the bias tape on top, your stitches should secure the underside as well.

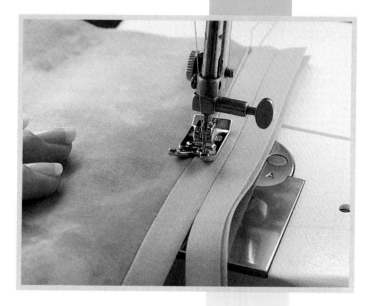

Repeat steps 8 and 9 for the remaining long edge, forming a large tube. If you have a **FREE ARM** on your machine, slip the excess fabric under the arm, through the opening. If you are stitching on a **FLAT BED** machine, be sure to maneuver the tube out of the way so that it is not caught in the stitching.

continued

continued

11 Turn the fabric tube wrong side out. Mark the center of the lower edge, opposite the joined tapes. Fold the lower edge flat, matching the center mark to the center of the bias tapes. Pin the edges together, inserting the pins perpendicular to the edges.

12 Place the fabric under the presser foot, aligning the edges to the ½" (1.3 cm) *seam allowance guide (p. 57)* and the fold to the opening in the presser foot. The bulk of the fabric is to the left of the machine. Stitch the seam across the bottom, stopping to remove pins as you come to them.

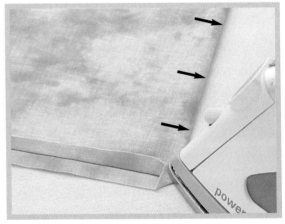

13 Press the seam flat, then turn back the top seam allowance and press, applying light pressure with the tip of the iron down the crease of the seam. Press creases in the lower 4" (10 cm) of the folded sides (arrows). (You'll understand the reason for this in the next step.)

14 Separate the front and back at one corner, forming a triangle by aligning the seamline to the creased fold on the side. Pin through the seam and crease.

15 Measure along the seam and mark a point 4" (10 cm) from the corner. Draw a line through the point perpendicular to the seam, from fold to fold. This line will be 8" (20.5 cm) long. Sew along this line, backstitching a few stitches at the beginning and end.

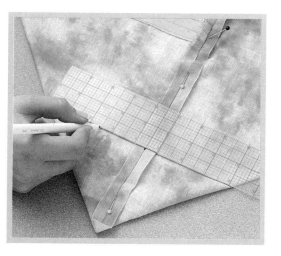

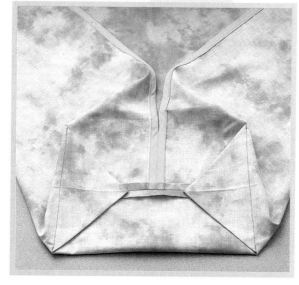

16 Repeat steps 14 and 15 for the other corner. Turn the triangles inward. You have now created the box corners that form the bottom of your diaper stacker.

continued

continued

17 With the stacker still turned wrong side out, fold and pin the upper edge as you did the lower edge in step 11. Mark a 2" (5 cm) line perpendicular to the upper edge 6" (15 cm) on each side of the center. Set the machine to stitch long straight stitches. **BASTE** the layers together on the marked lines.

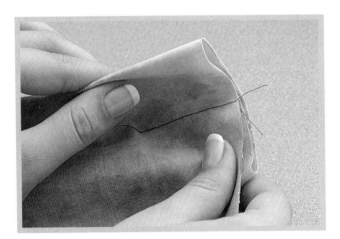

18 Open up the small circle of fabric formed between the basted line and the outer folded edge. Bring the fold line up to the basted line, and wrap the excess fabric around to the front and back. Pin through all the layers. Repeat on the other side.

19 Fold a tie in half. Slip it through the opening and position it up against the basted line, aligning the fold of the tie to the upper raw edges of the fabric; pin. Repeat for the other tie.

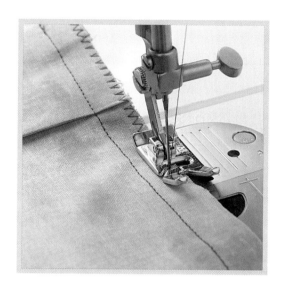

20 Stitch a seam through all layers across the upper edge, following the ½" (1.3 cm) seam allowance guide. Set the machine for a wide **ZIGZAG**, and *finish the raw edges together (p. 59).*

21 Turn the diaper stacker right side out. Remove the basting stitches at the sides, using a **SEAM RIPPER.** Do you see the neat **PLEATS** you've created at the upper corners? At the bottom, fold the triangular flaps toward each other, and insert the foam core board rectangle in the bottom to form a flat platform.

Give yourself a pat on the back!
Now simply tie the stacker to the crib railing or to a plastic hanger, if you prefer. Then load it up with diapers and you're ready for business!

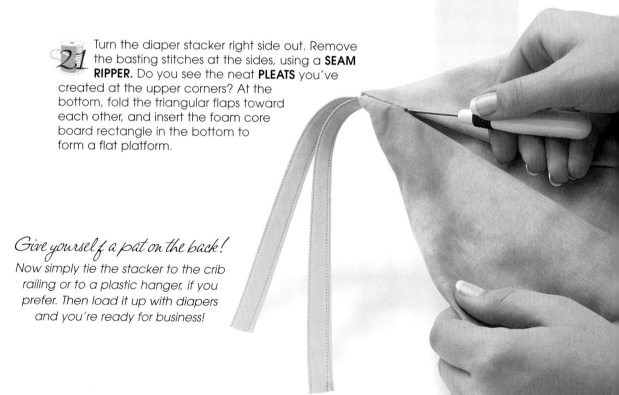

Bumper
Pad

Cushion the sides and ends of the crib with an easy-to-sew bumper pad. This unique design requires only simple sewing with overlap openings for inserting and removing the fabric-covered foam inserts. Polyurethane foam that is 1" (2.5 cm) thick is easy to cut with sewing shears, and it provides a firm protective padding. Look for fabric in a solid color or with a small **NONDIRECTIONAL PRINT** that can be **RAILROADED**. Then choose extra wide double-fold bias tape in a coordinating color for the ties.

WHAT YOU'LL LEARN

How to cut large
pieces of fabric
accurately

Sewing custom crib
decor is easier than
you thought!

How to use double-fold
bias tape for ties

WHAT YOU'LL NEED

5 yd. (4.6 m) fabric,
45" (115 cm) wide
or 3 yd. (2.75 m) fabric,
54" (137 cm) wide

54" (137 cm)
polyurethane foam,
1" (2.5 cm) thick and
24" (61 cm) wide

Quilting ruler or
carpenter's square

2½ yd. (2.3 m)
MUSLIN or similar
lightweight fabric for
covering foam

5 yd. (4.6 m) extra
wide double-fold
bias tape

Thread to match bias
tape and blend
with fabric

Let's Begin

1 Straighten the cut ends of the fabric, so they are perfectly perpendicular to the **SELVAGES.** Mark two rectangles, 26" (66 cm) wide and 1" (2.5 cm) longer than the inner crib side. Mark two rectangles, 26" (66 cm) wide and 1" (2.5 cm) longer than the inner crib end. Run the lengths on the **LENGTHWISE GRAIN.** *Do not use the selvage* as an edge. Use a quilter's ruler or carpenter's square for accuracy. Cut out the rectangles.

TIP: If your fabric is at least 54" (137 cm) wide, fold it in half lengthwise; mark one long and one short rectangle end to end. If the fabric is 45" (115 cm) wide, fold it in half crosswise; mark one long and one short rectangle end to end. Cut out both layers at once.

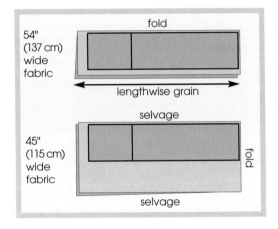

2 Pin one short and one long piece, right sides together, aligning the short ends. Insert the pins perpendicular to the edges. Place the fabric under the presser foot, with the bulk of the fabric to the left of the machine and the raw edges aligned to the 1/2" (1.3 cm) seam allowance guide. With the machine set on a straight stitch of 10 stitches per inch, or 2.5 mm, stitch the **SEAM.** Stop stitching and *remove pins as you come to them (pg. 49).*

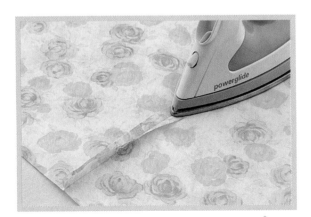

3 Repeat step 2 with the other set of rectangles. Then join the sets into one long strip, alternating sizes. The long rectangles are the bumper pad sides; the short pieces are the ends. *Press the seam allowances flat;* then press them open.

4 Press under 2" (5 cm) along one long side of the pieced strip. Unfold the pressed edge. Turn the cut edge back, aligning it to the first foldline; press the outer fold.

Quick Reference

Do not use the selvage. The tightly woven area along the outer edge of the fabric should be cut away in order to avoid puckering. Even if it looks flat, it would probably shrink and distort the shape of the bumper pad after laundering.

Press the seam allowances flat. The practice of pressing the seam flat first before pressing it open sets the stitches in the seamline and ultimately makes a better-looking seam.

5 Refold the edge along the pressed foldlines, encasing the raw edge to form a 1" (2.5 cm) **double-fold hem (pg. 55).** Pin the hem, inserting the pins perpendicular to the foldlines. Press and pin a 1" (2.5 cm) double-fold hem on the other long edge.

continued

continued

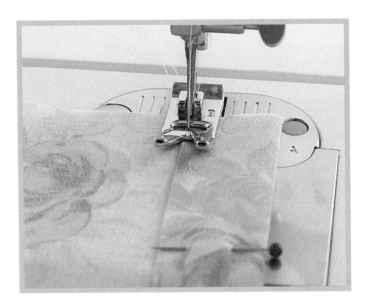

6 Place one pinned hem under the presser foot, with the wrong side of the fabric facing up and the bulk of the fabric to the left of the machine. Align the needle to enter the fabric just inside the inner fold, about ¼" (6 mm) from the short cut end.

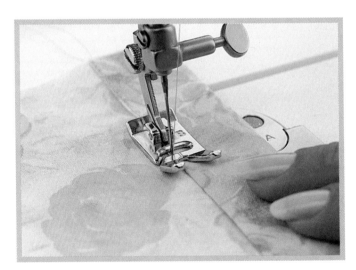

7 *Backstitch (pg. 19)* to the cut edge; then stitch forward, guiding the fabric so that the needle stitches on the edge of the fold. Stop stitching and remove pins as you come to them. Backstitch a few stitches at the opposite end.

8 Repeat steps 6 and 7 for the other hem. With the wrong side facing up, turn the lower hemmed edge up 5" (12.5 cm), and press the fold. Then fold the upper hemmed edge down, aligning it to the lower fold; press the upper fold. The folded fabric should now measure 8½" (21.8 cm) high.

9 Unroll the double-fold bias tape and press it lightly to remove any wrinkles. Cut five 24" (61 cm) pieces and four 12" (30.5 cm) pieces. **EDGESTITCH** next to the folds on both sides of the tape for each piece. This is shown in more detail in steps 3 and 4 on pages 62 and 63. Knot both ends of each long tie and one end of each short tie, if desired.

continued

continued

10 Unfold the fabric. On the right side of each short end, pin one short tie just below the top foldline and another just above the bottom foldline. Align the raw edges. Stitch and backstitch across the ties 3/8″ (1 cm) from the edges.

11 Fold the bumper pad strip at one end, right sides together, first folding the 8½″ (21.8 cm) top down and then folding the 5″ (12.7 cm) flap up. Align the raw edges, and pin. Make sure the ties extend inside away from the seam allowances. Stitch a ½″ (1.3 cm) seam across the end. Repeat at the opposite end.

Turn the bumper pad strip right side
out, and refold on the pressed foldlines;
press the ends. With the opening facing
up, draw a vertical line dividing each long
section in half. Pin the layers together at the
vertical seamlines and along the drawn lines.
Center a long tie across the top of each line.
Stitch through all layers at each seamline and
at the drawn lines, removing the pins as you
stitch. Backstitch over the tie and at the
bottom of each stitching line.

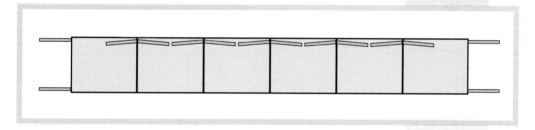

Prepare the foam inserts, as on
pages 78 and 79, steps 1 to 4.
Put the inserts into the bumper
pad cover, tucking them behind the
lower flap. Tie the bumper pad to
the crib rails, positioning the flap
opening to the outside.

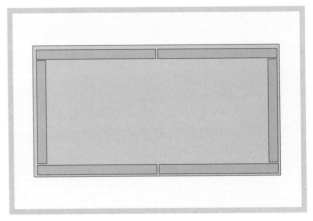

Let's Begin

1 ***Mark and cut six foam rectangles,*** all 8" (20.5 cm) wide. Cut four of them ½" (1.3 cm) shorter than half the inside length of the crib. Cut two of them 2" (5 cm) shorter than the inside width of the crib. The diagram above shows you how the foam pieces will fit inside the rails of the crib. Mark and cut six muslin rectangles, 30" x 19" (76 x 48.5 cm), for the covers.

2 Fold one cover in half lengthwise, right sides together, aligning the raw edges. Pin the layers together across one short end and the long raw edges, inserting the pins perpendicular to the edges. Stitch ½" (1.3 cm) seams where pinned, backstitching at the beginning and end, and **PIVOTING** with the needle down in the fabric at the corner. ***Trim off the corners of the seam allowances diagonally.*** Turn the cover right side out.

Quick Reference

Mark and cut foam rectangles. You can simply mark the foam with a pencil and cut it, using sewing shears.

Trim off the corners of the seam allowances diagonally. This minimizes the excess bulk to form a smoother corner when the piece is turned right side out.

3 Wrap a foam piece with lightweight plastic, and slip it into the cover. Remove the plastic. This is an easy, time-saving upholsterer's secret.

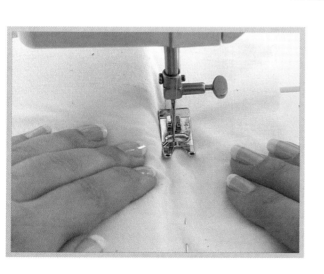

4 Pin the end closed, inserting the pins parallel to the end, with all the heads pointing down. Stitch the end closed, removing the pins as you come to them. Trim off the excess fabric, to within 1/4" (6 mm) of the stitches. **FINISH** the raw edges together using a **ZIGZAG** stitch.

Maybe sewing really is your forte!
After all, you just fashioned a major element for a totally coordinated crib ensemble, and now you're eager to sew more!

Nap-time Tote

When you take your baby for short visits, this convenient tote holds the essentials and zips open to provide a soft, cuddly surface for sleeping or playing. The tote is really a **LINED-TO-THE-EDGE** square. A handy lined pocket running from front to back provides extra cushion through the center. Purchase prequilted fabric for the outer layer and cotton flannel for the **LINING.** Be sure to **PRESHRINK** both fabrics before cutting and sewing. Look for a 30" (76 cm) molded **SEPARATING ZIPPER** in a color to coordinate with the fabric and lining.

WHAT YOU'LL LEARN

How to sew something that is lined to the edge

How to use paper-backed fusible web

How to **TOPSTITCH**

Zippers aren't as scary as you think!

WHAT YOU'LL NEED

Quilting ruler or carpenter's square for measuring and cutting

1¼ yd. (1.15 m) prequilted fabric

1¼ yd. (1.15 m) cotton flannel for lining

Thread to match or blend with the fabrics

Paper-backed fusible web, ⅜" (1 cm) wide

30" (76 cm) molded separating zipper

Basting tape

Point turner

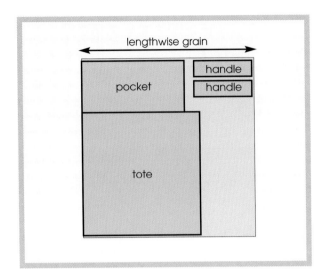

Let's Begin

1 Preshrink the fabric and lining. Using a quilter's ruler or a carpenter's square, mark out a perfect 31" (78.5 cm) square on the prequilted fabric, for the tote. Also measure and mark a 13" x 27" (33 x 68.5 cm) rectangle for the pocket and two 4" x 15" (10 x 38 cm) rectangles for the handles. ***Do not use a selvage as one of the sides (pg. 73).*** Cut out the pieces. Using the square and the pocket piece as patterns, cut matching pieces from the lining fabric.

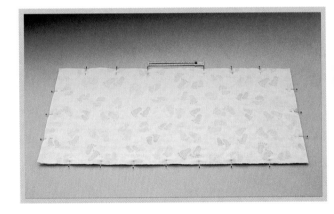

2 Pin the lining over the pocket, right sides together, around the entire outer edge. Insert the pins perpendicular to the edges. Leave a 6" (15 cm) opening unpinned along one side.

3 Set the machine for a straight stitch of 10 to 12 stitches per inch, or 2 to 2.5 mm. Place the pinned fabric under the presser foot just ahead of the opening. Align the cut edges to the 1/2" (1.3 cm) ***seam allowance guide (pg. 57)*** on the bed of the machine. The bulk of the fabric will extend to the left of the machine. ***Backstitch (pg 19)*** to the opening; stop. Then, stitch forward, guiding the cut edges along the 1/2" (1.3 cm) seam allowance guide. ***Remove pins as you come to them (pg. 49).*** Stop stitching 1/2" (1.3 cm) from the edge at the corner, leaving the needle down in the fabric. (Turn the handwheel until the needle is down.)

TIP: Mark a dot ½" (1.3 cm) from each corner on the wrong side of the lining. As you stitch toward each corner, you will be able to see exactly where you should stop.

4 Raise the presser foot and turn the fabric a quarter turn. Lower the presser foot and continue stitching. **PIVOT** in this manner at each corner. Stop stitching when you reach the last pin before the opening. Backstitch two or three stitches. *Remove the fabric from the machine (pg. 43).*

5 *Trim the seam allowances diagonally (pg. 79)* at the four corners. Press the seams flat to set the stitching line in the fabric. Insert a seam roll or wooden dowel into the opening and press the **SEAM ALLOWANCES** open over the curved surface. In the area of the opening, turn back the seam allowances ½" (1.3 cm) and press.

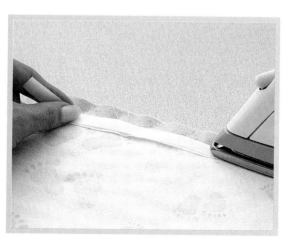

6 Cut a 6" (15 cm) strip of paper-backed fusible web. Place the strip over the lining seam allowance at the opening, just inside the folded edge. Press over the strip to fuse it to the seam allowance, following the manufacturer's directions.

continued

continued

7 Turn the pocket right side out through the opening. Insert a point turner or similar tool into the opening and gently push the pivot points out to form **perfect corners.** Remove the protective paper backing from the fusible web at the opening. Align the folded edges of the opening. Press over the opening from the lining side to fuse it closed. Press the remaining outer edges.

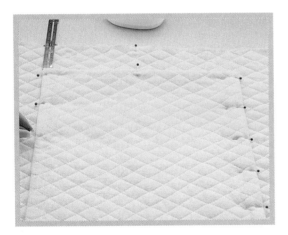

8 **MARK** the centers of two opposite sides of the tote piece; also mark the centers of the two short ends of the pocket. Center the pocket over the tote, right sides up. The pocket ends should be 2½" (6.5 cm) from the tote ends. Pin the pocket in place along both long edges, inserting pins perpendicular to the pocket edges.

9 Place the fabric under the presser foot so that the right edge of the foot is aligned to the side of the pocket and the back of the foot is aligned to the pocket end. Backstitch to the pocket end. Then, stitch forward to the opposite end; backstitch a few stitches. This is called **TOPSTITCHING.** Repeat for the opposite side of the pocket.

TIP: On most machines the right edge of the presser foot is ¼" (6 mm) from the needle tip. If this is not true of your machine, determine a different way to guide the stitching line ¼" (6 mm) from the pocket edge.

Perfect corners. The corners of your pocket should be sharply squared, not rounded. To improve the appearance of a slightly rounded corner, you can push a pointed utensil into the corner from inside to force the stitches out to the corner. An inexpensive specialty tool, called a point turner, works well; or you can use a large knitting needle, a ballpoint pen with the inkball retracted, or something similar. Use light pressure, though, so that you don't punch a hole in the corner.

10 Mark two lines across the pocket, each 1" (2.5 cm) from the center. Stitch on the marked lines, backstitching at each end of each line. This will divide the pocket into two. Mark and stitch a line down the center of one pocket side, to divide it for carrying bottles.

11 Press a handle piece in half lengthwise. Open the fold and turn the long edges in, aligning them to the center crease; press. Refold the center, encasing the raw edges. Pin the layers together. Repeat for the other handle. Topstitch 1/4" (6 mm) from both edges of each handle.

12 Pin the ends of one handle to the tote edge above one pocket, with the inner edges of the handle 3" (7.5 cm) from the center. Pin the other handle in the same position at the opposite edge. Stitch across the ends within the 1/2" (1.3 cm) seam allowance.

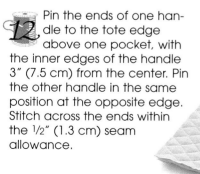

continued

13 Apply **basting tape** to the right side of the zipper tape, running it along both outer edges. Remove the protective paper backing.

14 Place the closed zipper facedown along one of the sides that doesn't have a handle, aligning the edges. The **zipper stops** at the top and bottom of the zipper should be 1/2" (1.3 cm) from the ends of the tote. Attach the zipper foot to the sewing machine, and adjust the machine so that the **needle will be stitching on the left side of the foot.** Set the machine for long straight stitches. **BASTE** the zipper tape to the fabric, stitching 3/8" (1 cm) from the edge.

TIP: Measure 3/8" (1 cm) from the outer edge of the zipper tape, and draw a guideline, using a pencil.

15 Adhere the other zipper tape edge to the opposite side of the tote as in step 14. Separate the zipper halves, and baste the other half in the same way. Pin the tote over the lining, right sides together, aligning all the edges and encasing the zipper and handles. Leave an opening between the handles on one end.

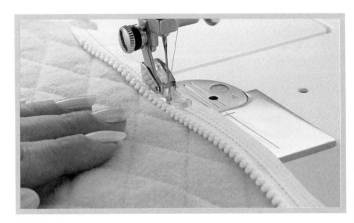

Place the fabric under the zipper foot, with the tote fabric on top, starting over one handle. Stitch ½" (1.3 cm) seam all around the tote, backstitching after and before the opening, and pivoting at the corners as in steps 2 and 3.

Trim the corners, press the seam allowances, turn the tote right side out, and close the opening as in steps 5 to 7 for the pocket. Attach the all-purpose presser foot. Topstitch ¼" (6 mm) from the edge all around the tote.

Quick Reference

Basting tape. This narrow tape is adhesive on both sides. As the tape comes off the roll, one side is sticky. After placing it on the zipper, remove the protective backing, exposing the other sticky side. Basting tape need not be removed after the zipper is stitched in place.

Zipper stops. Tiny bars at the top of the zipper prevent the zipper slide from sliding right off the end. On a separating zipper, the larger stop at the bottom secures and aligns the zipper teeth.

Needle will be stitching on the left side of the foot. On some machines, the needle position is adjustable; on others, the foot position is adjustable. Check your owner's manual for the correct way to set your machine.

Your tote is finished!

Simply zip it closed, fold it in half, and voila! . . . you're ready to go visiting.

Padded Wall Shapes

Dress up the walls of the nursery with fanciful padded shapes in various fabric colors and prints. Enlarge any of the patterns on pages 96 to 99 to the desired size, or draw simple shapes of your own. Give the shapes slight padding and support with 1/4" (6 mm) thick polyurethane foam, available at fabric or foam specialty stores. Use easy raw-edge **APPLIQUÉS** to add design features to the shapes, and embellish them with ribbons, rickrack, flat braids, buttons, or beads. Because the shapes are light-weight, they can be mounted to the wall using self-adhesive Velcro® dots.

WHAT YOU'LL LEARN

How to stitch neatly and accurately around curves

How to apply raw-edge appliqués

Stitching on foam is easier than you think!

WHAT YOU'LL NEED

Firmly woven, mediumweight fabrics in solid colors or small prints for fronts, backs, and appliqués

1/4" (6 mm) polyurethane foam, in a width suitable for your pattern (see step 1)

Paper-backed fusible web

Removable fabric marker

Flat braids, ribbons, rickrack, buttons, beads or other embellishments

Thread to match or blend with the fabrics and trims

Scrap of fusible interfacing

Self-adhesive Velcro dots

Let's Begin

1 Enlarge one of the patterns on pages 96 to 99, or **draw your own simple shape.** Cut out the pattern; also cut out any appliqué shapes. Cut rectangles of fabric for the front and back, allowing an ample margin around the shape. Also cut a matching rectangle of foam. Trace the outline of the pattern and any appliqué or trim placement onto the <u>wrong</u> side of the back fabric, using removable fabric marker. Repeat, marking on the <u>right</u> side of the front fabric.

TIP: To make the sewing easy, plan any flat trims to run in straight lines on the shape and extend to the outside of the shape so the ends can be caught in the outer **SEAM.**

2 Transfer the **mirror image** of any internal shapes onto the paper backing of paper-backed fusible web. Fuse the web to the wrong side of the appliqué fabric, **following the manufacturer's directions.**

3 Cut out the appliqué. Remove the paper backing. Fuse the appliqué onto the right side of the front fabric in the marked position, following the manufacturer's directions.

Draw your own simple shape. Avoid a shape that is wider than the foam, as it is difficult to join foam pieces invisibly. Also avoid any narrow extensions that will be difficult to turn right side out.

Mirror image. You must trace any directional shapes backward. When the appliqué is fused to the fabric it will appear forward.

Following the manufacturer's directions. When you buy paper-backed fusible web, such as Wonder Under®, the manufacturer's directions are printed continuously on a plastic wrapper throughout the bolt. Ask the person who cuts the web for you to also cut you off a set of directions.

4 Place any additional trims, such as ribbons, flat braids, or rickrack in the marked positions on the right side of the front piece; allow the ends to overlap the marked outer edge by ½" (1.3 cm). Hand-baste (page 36) the trims in place.

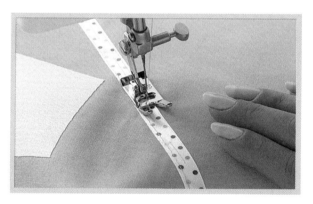

5 Set the machine for a straight stitch of 12 stitches per inch which equals 2 mm. Stitch the trims to the fabric, stitching down the center of narrow trims or rickrack. **EDGESTITCH** down both outer edges of wider trims and ribbons. Begin and end the stitching beyond the outer marked lines. Remove the basting.

6 Cut a 3" (7.5 cm) slit near the center of the back fabric. Place the front and back pieces right sides together. Check to see that the appliqués and trims on the front align to the placement marks on the back by holding the layers up to a light source.

continued

continued

7 Place the layers over the foam, with the wrong side of the back piece facing up. Pin the layers together around the outer marked line, with the pin heads pointing outward.

8 Place the layers under the presser foot, with the foam down. Align the needle to stitch on the marked line. Stitch around the entire shape, using short straight stitches. Stop stitching and **PIVOT** at corners. Stitch slowly around curves for best control.

TIP: Remember to let the machine feed the fabric while you simply guide the direction. For ease in stitching around sharp curves, stop every two or three stitches with the needle down in the fabric, raise the presser foot, and turn the fabric slightly. You may want to practice on scrap layers of fabric and foam before tackling your project.

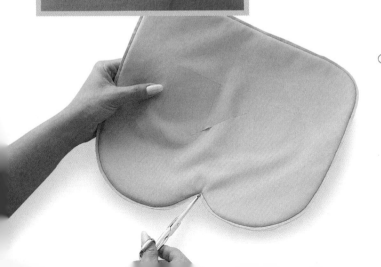

9 Trim the excess fabric and foam away to within ⅛" (3 mm) of the stitches. *Clip to, but not through,* the stitches at any inner corners.

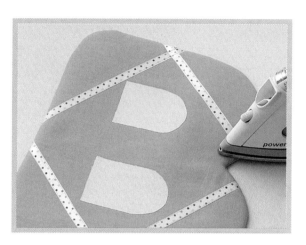

Clip to, but not through. This will allow the fabric to lay smoothly without puckering when the shape is turned right side out. Be careful not to cut the stitches, or a hole may develop in the seam.

10 Turn the shape right side out through the slit. Insert a point turner or similar tool into the opening and gently push any pivot points out to form **perfect corners (p. 85).** Push the seam out so that it is centered all around the outer edge. Press the outer edge lightly.

11 Cut a 4" (10 cm) strip of fusible interfacing, 1" (2.5 cm) wide. Slip it under the slit in the back fabric, fusible side up. Fuse the opening closed.

12 Straight-stitch around any appliqués through all the layers. Apply Velcro® dots to the back for hanging.

You just saved yourself some money!

Padded wall shapes that you buy in specialty shops can be a bit pricey. Now that you know you can do it yourself, plan a splashy arrangement of several shapes for the nursery.

MORE
Padded Shapes

Send the tortoise and the hare chasing across the wall. Build dimension by layering one padded shape over another, such as the hare's arm and leg, the tortoise's shell, and the butterfly's wings.

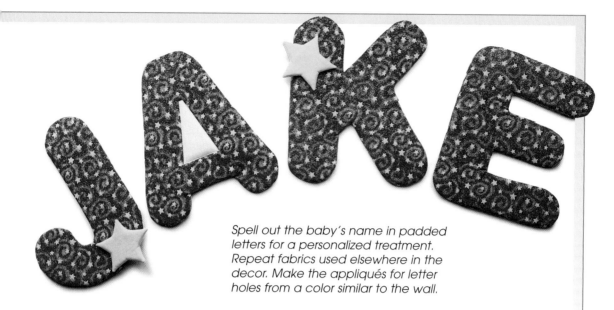

Spell out the baby's name in padded letters for a personalized treatment. Repeat fabrics used elsewhere in the decor. Make the appliqués for letter holes from a color similar to the wall.

Make the shapes from fabric printed with large motifs. On narrow extensions, like tails, be sure to leave enough room for turning the shape right side out; a cuticle stick or chop stick may be helpful. Emphasize the padded appearance with interior stitching lines.

ABCDE

KLMNO

TUVW

12345

F G H I J

P Q R S

X Y Z

6 7 8 9 0

Pieced-top Pillow

Toss a colorful, comfy pillow on the rocking chair for relaxing rock-a-bye sessions. Select a tightly woven cotton print fabric for the center square, four corner squares, and back. Then, drawing from colors in the print, select three coordinating cotton fabrics, in solid colors or tiny-grained prints for the remaining rectangles. You could cut all of these pieces using sewing shears; however, this is a great project for learning to use a **ROTARY CUTTER AND MAT.** The cutting and piecing techniques used for this pillow are basics for quilting, so if you have longed to become a quilter, this project could get you started.

Notice that 1/4" (6 mm) **SEAM ALLOWANCES** are used in the pillow top, which is the standard width for quilting. However, the seam allowances around the outer edge are 1/2" (1.3 cm), which will be easier for slipstitching the opening closed.

WHAT YOU'LL LEARN

How to cut fabric using a rotary cutter and mat

How to match **SEAMS** with precision

Careful pressing really does matter

How to slipstitch

WHAT YOU'LL NEED

1/2 yd. (0.5 m) multicolor, tightly woven cotton fabric

1/8 yd. (0.15 m) each of three coordinating fabrics

Rotary cutter and mat

Quilting ruler

Thread to match or blend with the fabrics

14" (35.5 cm) square pillow form

Let's Begin

1 Fold the printed fabric in half lengthwise; smooth it out on the surface of the cutting mat, aligning the **SELVAGES** *on a horizontal grid line.* (The cut ends may not align.) Place the quilter's ruler over the fabric, perpendicular to the fold and selvages, with the ruler edge near the cut ends on one side. Holding the ruler firmly in place with one hand, trim the excess fabric off along the ruler edge, using the rotary cutter. Apply steady, firm pressure to the blade. Shift your hand position on the ruler as necessary, making sure the fabric and ruler do not move out of position.

TIP: If you are right-handed, hold the ruler with your left hand and cut with the right hand, guiding the blade of the cutter along the right edge of the ruler. If you are left-handed, do just the opposite.

2 Reposition the folded fabric on the cutting mat with the straightened end on a horizontal grid line. Place the ruler over the fabric perpendicular to the cut end, with the ruler edge just inside the selvages. *Trim off the selvages,* using the rotary cutter.

3 Unfold the fabric and align two straightened edges to the grid lines on the cutting mat. Carefully measure and **MARK** the corners for a 15" (38 cm) square, using the two cut edges for two sides of the square. Align the quilting ruler to the marks, and hold it firmly in place. Cut the fabric, guiding the rotary cutter along the ruler edge. Cut a 6½" (16.3 cm) square in the same way.

On a horizontal grid line. The measured grid on the surface of the cutting mat is not only handy for measuring, but more importantly as a guide for cutting perfect square corners. With the selvages on a horizontal grid line, you can line the ruler up to a vertical grid line to straighten the cut ends.

4 Align the 4¾" (12 cm) line on the ruler to the straightened edge on the remaining print fabric. Cut a strip. You may have to shift the fabric so that it lies on the same side as the hand holding the cutter. Cut four 4¾" (12 cm) squares from the strip.

5 Straighten the cut ends and remove the selvages on the other three fabrics, as in steps 1 and 2. Unfold one fabric and cut a 2½" (6.5 cm) strip from the straightened end, half the width of the fabric. Repeat for the other fabrics.

6 Pin the light and medium value strips, right sides together, along one edge, aligning the upper ends. (The lower ends may not align.) Place the fabric under the presser foot with the upper ends aligned to the needle hole in the throat plate. Align the cut edges to the 1/4" *(6 mm) seam allowance guide (pg. 49).* Stitch the 1/4" (6 mm) seam, *removing pins as you come to them (pg. 49).*

continued

continued

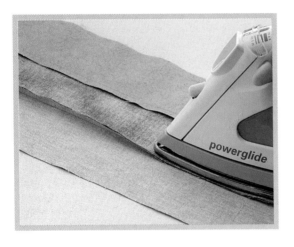

 7 Stitch the darkest strip to the other side of the medium value strip. **PRESS** all the seam allowances toward the darkest strip.

TIP: You can sew these strips together without pinning first, if you take your time. Keep the edges aligned and hold both strips with even tension. The strips may not be exactly the same length. Start with the ends evenly aligned and begin stitching from that same end with both seams.

8 If you stitched accurate 1/4" (6 mm) seams, the pieced strip should measure 6½" (16.3 cm) across. Cut the pieced strip crosswise into four 4¾" (12 cm) pieces.

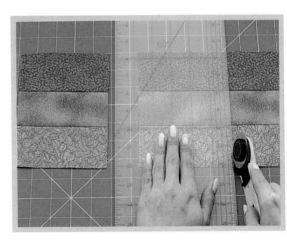

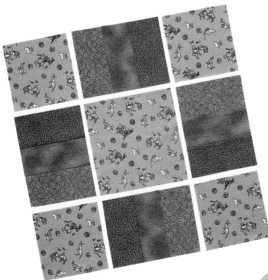

9 Arrange the blocks for the pillow top into three rows as shown. Stitch the seams to join the blocks of each row together, taking the blocks in order from the surface.

10 Press the new seam allowances for the top and bottom rows away from the corner squares. Press the new seam allowances for the middle row away from the center square.

Quick Reference

Inserting pins in the wells of the seams.
By pinning directly through the seam stitches, you are making sure that the stitched seams will line up perfectly on the right side of the pillow. Stitch up to these pins as close as you can before removing them.

11 Pin the top row to the middle row, right sides together and raw edges even. Align the seams, *inserting pins in the wells of the seams.* You will notice that the matching seam allowances turn in opposite directions. Stitch a 1/4" (6 mm) seam, removing the pins as you come to them.

TIP: To ensure perfect intersections, slow down as you approach each one. Stop with the needle down in the fabric, raise the presser foot, and lift the fabrics slightly from the machine bed. Make sure the seam allowances on the underside are still turned in the direction they were pressed. Then lower the presser foot and continue stitching.

12 Pin the bottom row to the opposite side of the middle row, pinning as in step 11; stitch the seam. Press both new seam allowances away from the center. You have just completed the pillow front.

continued

continued

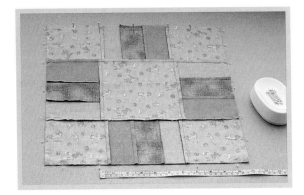

13 Place the pillow front over the pillow back, right sides together, and align all four edges. Pin the layers together near the outer edges, inserting the pins perpendicular to the edges. In the center of one side, leave a 7" (18 cm) opening unpinned.

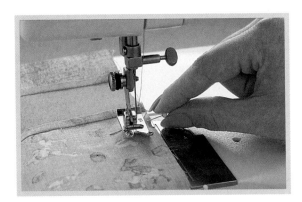

14 Place the fabric under the presser foot, just ahead of the opening. Align the cut edges of the fabric to the 1/2" (1.3 cm) seam allowance guide on the bed of the machine. Remove the pin that marks the opening before lowering the presser foot.

15 *Backstitch (pg. 19)* three or four stitches; stop. Then, stitching forward, stitch the seam on all four sides, **PIVOTING** with the needle down at the corners. End the seam by backstitching three or four stitches at the opposite side of the opening.

16 Remove the fabric from the machine. Trim the threads close to the fabric. Press the seams flat to set the stitching line in the fabric. Then, turn back the top seam allowance and press, applying light pressure with the tip of the iron down the crease of the seam. In the opening, turn back and press the seam allowances 1/2" (1.3 cm).

17 Turn the pillow cover right side out. Insert a point turner or similar tool into the opening to gently force the stitches out to the corners.

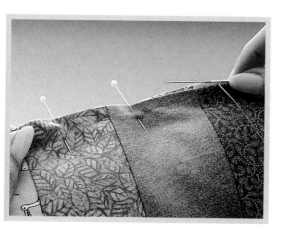

18 Compress and insert the pillow form. Align the pressed edges of the opening, and pin the opening closed. Thread a hand needle and tie a knot in the end (page 36). Slipstitch the opening closed, following the instructions on page 37.

Now you are an experienced pillow maker!
And, you've just had a little taste of what could be in store for you if you decide to pursue the exciting world of quilting.

MORE
Pieced-pillow
OPTIONS

Create a memory pillow by transferring a photo of your baby to white fabric, for the center square. Follow the transfer paper manufacturer's directions or have the photo transferred to fabric at a copy shop. Select other fabrics in colors that compliment the photograph. Write birth information on the narrow strips, using fabric pens.

Use fabrics with various textures, including cotton flannel, robe velour, satin, and corduroy. Your baby will be fascinated by the tactile sensations on those tiny fingertips.

Cut individual print motifs from a fine-wale corduroy print for the center and corner squares. Select corduroy in colors drawn from the print for the narrow strips.

Window Topper

This easy stylish window topper has lots of creative possibilities. Designed as a decorative accent over a shade or blinds, it is simply a flat **LINED-TO-THE-EDGE** shape that flips over a decorative rod. Buttonholes and buttons secure the topper and add a splash of color. A layer of lining fabric between the front and back fabrics, called **INTERLINING,** adds body and support for the buttonholes. Because you first create a paper pattern, you can design the topper with straight, curved, or pointed lower edges. Select firmly woven fabrics in two coordinating colors or a **NONDIRECTIONAL PRINT** and a solid color, one for the front and one for the back.

WHAT YOU'LL LEARN

If you can measure, draw lines, and cut paper, you can design a window topper!

How to sew buttonholes and buttons

How to sew something that is lined to the edge

WHAT YOU'LL NEED

Decorative curtain rod

Two coordinating firmly woven fabrics, amount determined after making pattern

Drapery lining fabric, amount determined after making pattern

Wide craft paper

Quilting ruler or carpenter's square

Thread to blend with the fabrics

Buttons in desired sizes and colors

Liquid fray preventer

Buttonhole cutter

111

Let's Begin

1 Mount the rod so that the top is even with the top of the window frame or slightly higher. The brackets should be just outside the frame or at least 1" (2.5 cm) beyond any existing treatment. Measure from bracket to bracket to determine the width of the topper pattern. Hang a tape measure over the rod to determine the length of the pattern.

TIP: The topper should be at least long enough to cover a raised blind or shade. For a pleasing proportion, it should cover no more than one-third of the window.

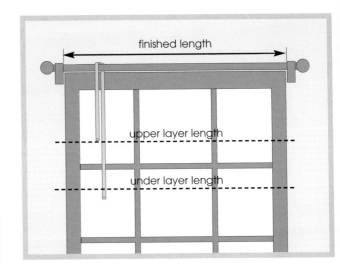

finished length

upper layer length

under layer length

2 Cut a paper pattern to these dimensions, using a quilting ruler or carpenter's square for accuracy. Shape the lower edges into one or more shallow curves or points, if you desire, and hang it over the rod. Stand back for a look, and make any final adjustments. Draw a line where the pattern crosses the rod. Measure the pattern and buy equal amounts of both fabrics and the interlining. **PRESHRINK** all three fabrics if you intend to launder the topper.

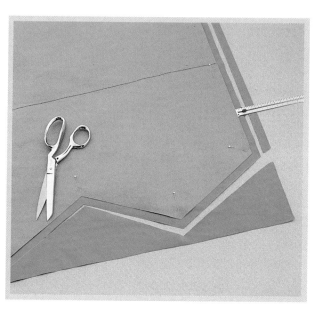

Quick Reference

Leave the pins in the fabric. The layers are already aligned and pinned to begin sewing.

TIP: If the window is narrower than the fabric, purchase slightly more fabric than the pattern length. You will align the pattern vertically to the **LENGTH-WISE GRAIN** of the fabric. If the window is wider than the fabric, purchase slightly more fabric than the pattern width. You will align the pattern vertically to the **CROSSWISE GRAIN.**

3 Pin the pattern over one of the fabrics. The outer edge of the pattern is the stitching line for the topper. Mark the cutting line on the fabric, 1/2" (1.3 cm) beyond the pattern edge. Cut out the fabric. Remove the pattern.

4 Place the other fabric face-up over the interlining. Pin the cut fabric facedown over both layers, aligning all grainlines. Insert the pins near and perpendicular to the cut edges. Cut the other layers. **Leave the pins in the fabric.**

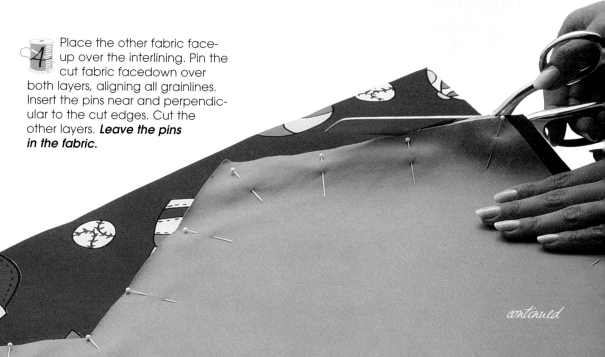

continued

continued

5 Set the machine for a straight stitch of 12 stitches per inch, which equals 2 mm. Place the fabric under the presser foot near the center of one long edge, so that the cut edges are aligned to the 1/2" (1.3 cm) **seam allowance guide (pg. 57). Backstitch (pg. 19)** a few stitches. Then stitch forward, guiding the cut edges along the 1/2" (1.3 cm) seam allowance guide. **Remove pins as you come to them (pg. 49).**

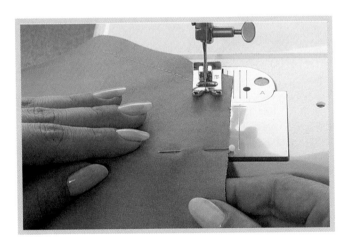

6 Stop stitching at the first corner, leaving the needle down in the fabric. (Turn the handwheel until the needle is down.) Raise the presser foot, and turn the fabric. Lower the presser foot, and continue stitching. **PIVOT** in the same way at each corner.

7 Stop stitching about 10" (25.5 cm) from where you began; back-stitch, leaving an opening for turning the topper right side out. **Remove the fabric from the machine (pg. 43). Trim the seam allowances diagonally at outer corners (pg. 79). Clip to, but not through (pg. 93),** the stitches at any inner corners.

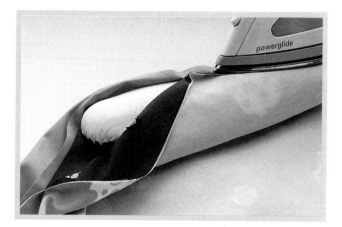

8 **PRESS** the seams flat to set the stitching line in the fabric. Insert a heavy cardboard tube or a seam roll (page 25) into the opening. Press the seam allowances open, applying light pressure with the tip of the iron down the crease of the seam.

9 Turn back the seam allowances 1/2" (1.3 cm) along the opening, and press. (On one side you will also be turning back the interlining.) Cut a 10" (25.5 cm) strip of 3/8" (1 cm) paper-backed fusible web. Place the strip over the seam allowance at the opening, just inside the folded edge. Press over the strip to fuse it to the seam allowance, following the manu-facturer's directions.

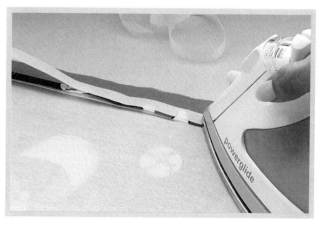

continued

continued

10 Turn the valance right side out through the opening. Insert a point turner or similar tool into the opening and gently push any pivot points out to form ***perfect corners (p. 85).*** Push the seam out so that it is centered all around the outer edge. Press the entire valance. Remove the protective paper backing from the fusible web at the opening. Align the folded edges of the opening. Press over the opening to fuse it closed.

11 Place the topper on a flat surface. Using the marked line on the pattern as a guide, fold the upper flap down. Plan and mark the placement for vertical buttonholes, keeping the lower ends of the buttonholes at least 1" (2.5 cm) above the lower edge of the flap. Mark lines that equal the diameter plus the thickness of the buttons.

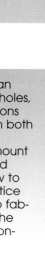

TIP: If you prefer, you can opt not to make buttonholes, and simply sew the buttons onto the topper through both layers. Then slip the rod through the topper to mount it. However, this is a good opportunity to learn how to make buttonholes. Practice on a triple layer of scrap fabric until you are sure of the technique and the buttonhole length.

12 Attach your buttonhole presser foot or buttonhole attachment. Follow the instructions in your owner's manual to stitch the buttonholes over the marked lines. Apply liquid fray preventer to the buttonholes; allow it to dry. Cut the buttonholes open, using a buttonhole cutter (page 27) or small, sharp scissors.

13 Refold the topper. Mark the placements for the buttons on the lower layer, inserting the marker through the bottom of each buttonhole. Sew the buttons to the topper, as on page 38 or 39. Hang the window topper over the rod.

You should be pretty impressed with yourself!
Not only did you sew a window treatment, you also designed it and created the pattern. Just think of the possibilities!

MORE
Window Topper
OPTIONS

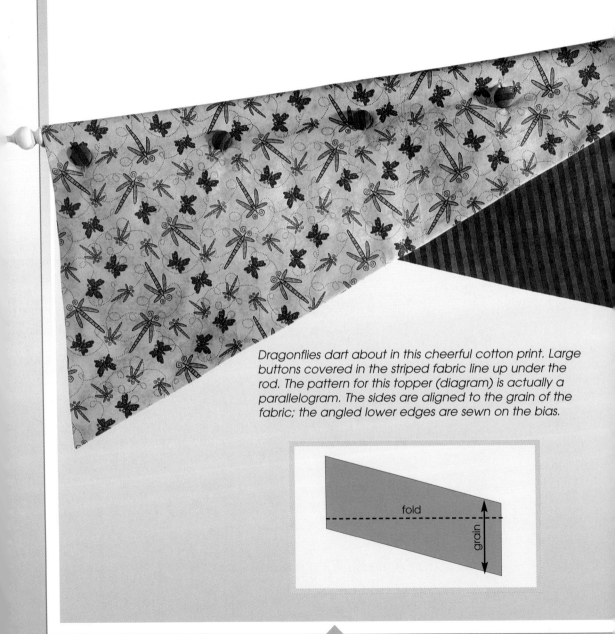

Dragonflies dart about in this cheerful cotton print. Large buttons covered in the striped fabric line up under the rod. The pattern for this topper (diagram) is actually a parallelogram. The sides are aligned to the grain of the fabric; the angled lower edges are sewn on the bias.

fold

grain

*The colors of soft
pastel stripes are repeated
with fancy balloon buttons positioned
along the angled lower edges. Sew buttonholes along the grainline, even though
the edge runs on the bias.*

*Curved seam allowances are trimmed to ¼" (6 mm) for ease in turning right side
out. Ribbon ties are cut 18" (46 cm) long and stitched to the under layer instead of
buttons. The ribbon ends are then pulled through small buttonholes and tied into
bows, anchoring the topper over the pole.*

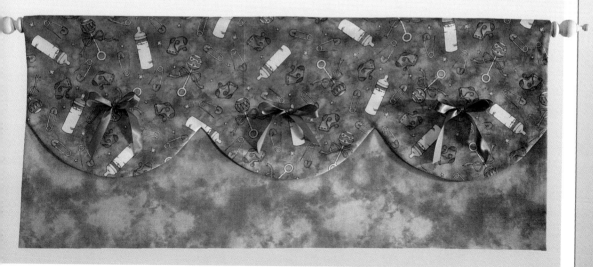

MORE
Creative Ideas

Decorate the window topper with padded shapes. Perhaps use scraps of fabric left over from other elements of the nursery decor to tie it all together. Secure the shapes with hand stitches.

Hand-baste pregathered lace trim to the front edges of a diaper stacker before encasing them with the double-fold bias tape. Sew a padded shape to mount over the top of the stacker. Simply tie the stacker to a plastic hanger and then attach the shape to the hanger, using Velcro® dots.

For extra cushion, sew a bumper pad from prequilted fabric. Use grosgrain ribbon for the ties. Sew lined-to-the-edge pockets at the head section to tuck away an extra pacifier, teething ring, or small stuffed toys.

Glossary

APPLIQUÉ. This French word refers to a decoration or cutout that is applied to the surface of a larger piece of fabric. Many methods of appliqué are used, including simply machine stitching around the outline of the decoration or hand stitching invisibly.

BACKSTITCH. Several stitches are taken in the reverse direction at the beginning and end of a seam to keep the stitching line from pulling out.

BASTING. Long, easy-to-remove stitches are sewn into the fabric temporarily, either by hand or by machine. Hand-basting stitches are used to hold layers of fabric and batting together for quilting. They are also used to gather a section of fabric into a smaller space. Machine-basting stitches are used to close a seam before inserting a zipper.

BASTING TAPE. Narrow tape that is sticky on both sides holds two pieces of fabric together so they will not shift while you are sewing.

BIAS. Any diagonal line intersecting the lengthwise and crosswise grains of fabric is referred to as *bias*. While woven fabric does not stretch on the lengthwise and crosswise grains, it has considerable stretch on the bias.

BOBBINS. Sewing machines form stitches by interlocking an upper thread with a lower thread. The lower thread is wound on a small spool, or *bobbin*, designed specifically for that machine.

BUILT-IN BUTTONHOLER. Some machines are capable of making a buttonhole without the use of a separate attachment.

CASING. A fabric tunnel is sewn into an item, usually along an edge, to carry elastic or cording.

CHALK. Several forms of chalk are available for marking guidelines and points on fabric. Chalk marks can be easily brushed off the fabric when they are no longer needed.

CROSSWISE GRAIN. On woven fabric, the crosswise grain runs perpendicular to the selvages. Fabric has slight "give" in the crosswise grain.

EDGESTITCH. With the machine set for straight stitching at a length of 2 to 2.5 mm or 10 to 12 stitches per inch, stitch within 1/8" (3 mm) of a finished edge. With many machines, this can be achieved by guiding the inner edge of the right presser foot toe along the outer finished edge.

FLAT BED. The bed of the sewing machine is flush with the cabinet or sewing surface.

FREE ARM. Many sewing machines are designed with a narrow, free-standing bed that allows for easy access to tight areas and for sewing inside a cylinder. Fabric can wrap completely around the free arm.

FULLNESS describes the finished width of a fabric piece in proportion to the length of the flat piece to which it is being sewn. For example, two times fullness means that the width at the lower edge of a crib skirt measures twice the width of the deck to which it is sewn.

GATHERING. Excess fabric is drawn into closely spaced puckers along a line of stitching to create a design feature while controlling fullness. For home decorating items, this is often done by zigzagging over a strong cord and then sliding the fabric along the cord to gather the fabric.

INTERLINING is a layer of fabric encased between the top fabric and the lining for the purpose of preventing light from shining through or to add body to the item, as for a window topper. Interlining is usually plain white or ecru, such as drapery lining fabric.

LENGTHWISE GRAIN. On woven fabric, the lengthwise grain runs parallel to the selvages. It is the strongest direction of the fabric with the least amount of "give."

LINED TO THE EDGE means that a fabric panel is backed with lining that is cut to the exact same size. The two pieces are joined together by a seam around the outer edge.

LINING is a fabric backing sewn to the top fabric to provide extra body, protection from sunlight, and support for side hems.

MARKING. It is often necessary to give yourself temporary guidelines or guide points on the fabric for cutting or matching seams. There are many tools and methods for doing this, such as marking pencils and pens, chalk dispensers, tape, or simply using pins.

MITERED. Excess fabric is folded out at an angle to eliminate bulk. You probably miter the corners when you wrap gifts.

MULTISTITCH-ZIGZAG. Depending on your sewing machine brand, this stitch may also be called a "serpentine" or "darning" stitch. The needle moves from left to right, taking multiple stitches in each direction, rather than the one stitch in each direction taken by a standard zigzag stitch.

MUSLIN. This plain, lightweight, firmly woven cotton fabric is usually either white or unbleached. Because it is relatively inexpensive, it is often used in areas where it serves a purpose, but will not be seen, such as the deck of a crib skirt.

NONDIRECTIONAL PRINT. The design printed on the fabric has no definite "up" and "down" directions, so the project can be cut with the crosswise grain running up and down.

PIVOT. Perfect corners are stitched by stopping with the needle down in the fabric at the exact corner, before turning the fabric. To be sure the corner stitch locks, turn the handwheel until the needle goes all the way down and just begins to rise.

PLEATS. Fabric is deliberately folded to one side and sewn in place to create a design feature while controlling excess fullness.

PRESHRINKING. Fabric that shrinks, especially natural fibers, shrinks most in the first laundering. If you intend to launder your finished item occasionally, you should wash the fabric before cutting out the pieces, so the item will not shrink after you make it. "Dry clean only" fabrics usually don't shrink as much, but can be preshrunk by steaming them with your iron.

PRESSING. This step is extremely important to the success of your sewing projects. Select the heat setting appropriate for your fabric and use steam. Lift and lower the iron in an overlapping pattern. Do not slide the iron down the seam, as this can cause the fabric to stretch out of shape, especially on the crosswise grain or bias.

RAILROADING. The lengthwise grain of the fabric is run horizontally, eliminating the need for vertical seams and often conserving fabric. Railroading is only suitable for nondirectional prints or solid-colored fabrics.

ROTARY CUTTER AND MAT. This time-saving method of cutting fabric may also take a little practice and serious precautions. The blade on a rotary cutter is extremely sharp. Cut slowly, watch your fingers, and <u>always</u> retract or cover the blade between cuts. The rotary cutter cannot be used without the special mat.

SEAM. Two pieces of fabric are placed right sides together and joined along the edge with stitches. After stitching, the raw edges are hidden on the wrong side, leaving a clean, smooth line on the right side.

SEAM ALLOWANCE. Narrow excess fabric, 1/2" (1.3 cm) for most of the projects in this book, lies between the stitching line and the raw edge. Stitching with a 1/2" (1.3 cm) seam allowance gives the seam strength and ensures that the stitches cannot be pulled off the raw edges.

SEAM RIPPER. It doesn't really rip. Use the sharp point to slide under and cut stitches one at a time. Avoid the temptation to simply slide the cutting hook down the seam. You will inevitably cut into your fabric. Even the most experienced sewers rely on their seam rippers.

SELVAGE. Characteristic of woven fabrics, this narrow, tightly woven outer edge should be cut away. Avoid the temptation to use it as one side of a cut piece, as it may cause the seam to pucker and may shrink excessively when washed.

SEPARATING ZIPPER. Zippers that come completely apart at the bottom are intended for use in items like jackets or the tote on page 81. Check the label carefully in the store, to be sure you are buying the correct zipper style.

SLIP STITCH. This versatile hand stitch is useful for many tasks, such as closing the opening on a pillow, after inserting the pillow form. Done well, a slipstitched opening is as invisible as the machine-sewn seams on either side of it.

STRAIGHT STITCH. Your machine forms stitch after stitch in a straight row because the needle does not change its position in this setting. You can alter the length of the stitch from long basting stitches to stitching in place. What you are really changing is the amount of fabric the feed dogs move with each stitch.

STRETCH STITCH. Differing among sewing machine brands, these stitches are designed to "lengthen" as the fabric stretches. Some stitch styles are a combination of zigzag and straight stitches that stitch and finish the seam in one pass.

TACKING. Short stationary stitches, sewn either by hand or by machine, hold two pieces of fabric together.

TENSION. When your machine puts the same amount of "pull" on both the top thread and the bobbin thread, your stitches lock exactly halfway between the top and bottom of the fabric layers. Even tension is essential for successful sewing. Some sewing machines require minor tension adjustments when switching from one fabric to another.

TOPSTITCH. A decorative and functional stitching line placed 1/4" to 1" (6 mm to 2.5 cm) from the finished edge of an item. The stitching is done with the right side of the item facing up. Sometimes topstitching is done with a heavier thread or two threads through the machine needle, to make it more visible.

ZIGZAG STITCH. In this setting, the needle alternately moves from left to right with each stitch. You can alter the width of the needle swing as well as the length of the stitch. A zigzag stitch that is twice as wide as it is long gives you a balanced stitch, appropriate for finishing the edge of a seam.

Index